MAN'S FAITH
AND FREEDOM

MAN'S FAITH AND FREEDOM

THE THEOLOGICAL INFLUENCE OF JACOBUS ARMINIUS

Edited by
Gerald O. McCulloh

Wipf & Stock
PUBLISHERS
Eugene, Oregon

Wipf and Stock Publishers
199 W 8th Ave, Suite 3
Eugene, OR 97401

Man's Faith and Freedom
The Theological Influence of Jacobus Arminius
Edited by McCulloh, Gerald O.
ISBN 13: 978-1-55635-160-0
ISBN 10: 1-55635-160-7
Publication date 12/22/2006
Previously published by Abingdon, 1962

FOREWORD

This book contains the addresses delivered in the Arminius Symposium held at Amsterdam, Leiden, and Utrecht, in Holland, August 4-7, 1960. The Remonstrant Brotherhood sponsored the Symposium as a part of a national celebration of the fourhundredth anniversary of the birth of Jacobus Arminius.

The Arminius Symposium brought together from various parts of the Christian world about 250 representatives of the free churches in which Arminian influence is discernible. As a theologian who emphasized the doctrinal principles of universality and freedom, Arminius' teachings and spirit have been highly influential in many free-church movements since the time of the Protestant Reformation. Emerging as he did in the time of the struggle which resulted in the establishment of Protestantism, his writings may well be included in the revival of theological studies of the Reformation writings. Standing as he did in opposition to some of the doctrinal and ecclesiastical developments of Calvinism and the Reformed Church, Arminius supplies important insights into the struggle for freedom and toleration. As a champion of variety in unity within the church and an irenical concern in theology, Arminius' writings should be studied by all who seek the extension of Christian unity through the ecumenical movement.

The Remonstrant Brotherhood (*Remonstrantse Broederschap*) was begun informally in 1610, a year after Arminius' death, to present a "remonstrance" to the States of Holland in which were included a request for a General Synod to settle the theological disputes dividing the country and a challenge to the prevailing Calvinist theology at five points: unconditional predestination, limited atonement, man's ability to exercise faith, irresistible grace, and the perseverance of the saints. Although the Remonstrant Brotherhood refused the name "Arminian," yet their principles were clearly rooted in Arminius' theology. The Synod of Dort (*Dordrecht*) in 1618-19, convened in response to this call, condemned the Remonstrants, banished their leaders, and put one of the partisans to death. The leaders in exile, however, rallied their followers, returned secretly to Holland, and extended their Brotherhood when the official ban was relaxed a decade later. The Remonstrant Brotherhood has continued uninterruptedly its life as a free church, holding a doctrine of free grace and working for the freedom of man in a free Christian society.

The Arminius Symposium met for its several sessions in the Arminius Church in Amsterdam, the theological lecture hall at the University of Leiden, Pieters Church, Leiden, where Arminius is buried, and the Geerte Church, Utrecht. The members of the Symposium also visited Oudewater, Arminius' birthplace, where an outstanding exhibition of manuscripts, pictures, and early publications had been arranged as a feature of the national observance of the four-hundredth anniversary.

Gerrit Jan Hoenderdaal is professor of Arminian theology at Leiden University. Lambertus Jacobus van Holk is professor of philosophy of religion at Leiden University. Geoffrey F. Nuttall is a pastor in the Congregational Church in London. James Luther Adams is professor of Christian ethics in Harvard Divinity School, Harvard University. Russell Henry Stafford, who preached the sermon in the International Service at the Geerte Church, Utrecht, is moderator of the International Congregational Council.

The editor extends grateful thanks to the authors for the several papers, to the Remonstrant Brotherhood for sponsoring the Arminius Symposium, for making the manuscripts available, and for many courtesies of hospitality extended to these sharing in the Symposium, especially to Mrs. T. B. M. van Beusekom, the General Secretary of the Remonstrant Brotherhood.

GERALD O. McCULLOH, EDITOR

CONTENTS

1. The Life and Struggle of Arminius in the Dutch Republic
   —Gerrit Jan Hoenderdaal 11
2. From Arminius to Arminianism in Dutch Theology
   —Lambertus Jacobus van Holk 27
3. The Influence of Arminianism in England
   —Geoffrey F. Nuttall 46
4. The Influence of Arminius on American Theology
   —Gerald O. McCulloh 64
5. Arminius and the Structure of Society
   —James Luther Adams 88
6. Faith and Wonder
   —Russell Henry Stafford 113
   Bibliography 119
   Index 125

[1] The Life and Struggle of Arminius in the Dutch Republic

Gerrit Jan Hoenderdaal *

It would be fruitless to attempt a discussion of the life of Jacobus Arminius without first considering the political and ecclesiastical situation of his day. For instance, his early youth was deeply influenced by the turbulent events which inaugurated the great fight of the Dutch people for their liberation from the Spanish yoke. Resentment against the repressive religious and civil policies of Philip II had erupted in armed revolt by 1566. Led by William, Prince of Orange, also known as William the Silent, the resistance was to continue until 1609. Closely related to this struggle was the position of the Reformed Church in Holland. In 1523 the first martyrs for the cause had been burned at the stake in Brussels, then the capital of the Netherlands. Soon afterwards, several Protestant trends manifested themselves, variously inspired by Luther, Erasmus, and the Anabaptists. When Arminius was born in 1560, Calvinism was in its initial stages. Calvin's Academy at Geneva had only been in existence for a year, and his *Institutes* had just appeared in their final version. In Holland there was developing a specifically Dutch Reformation, the character of which eventually proved to be more inti-

* This chapter has been rewritten for publication, and appears in this form by permission of the author.

mately connected with Melanchthon and Bullinger than with Luther and Calvin.

In 1575 the Spaniards burned Arminius' native town of Oudewater. Although he had only recently been registered as a student in Marburg University, he returned to his country at once and found that his mother and his brothers had been killed. His father having died during his infancy, Arminius found himself without a family. He soon found refuge, however, in the house of Peter Bertius, a minister of the Reformed Church in Rotterdam.

Leiden University had just been established as a reward for the courageous resistance of the townspeople when the city lay under siege. Arminius, together with the son of Bertius, now matriculated there as a student of divinity and soon distinguished himself. Recognizing him as a potential leader of the Reformed Church, the Merchant Guild of the city of Amsterdam sent him, at their expense, to the Academy at Geneva. This event, taking place in 1581 when Arminius was twenty-one years old, is particularly revealing in showing the influence Calvinism was beginning to have in the Netherlands: the Geneva Academy was already being considered as the chief Reformed university in Europe.

Here Arminius came under the influence of Théodore de Bèze, who lectured in dogmatics and exegesis, and of a number of professors in the field of philosophy. Concerning the latter, A. W. Harrison writes:

> The study of Logic proved to be more controversial than that of Theology at Geneva. There Aristotle reigned supreme with his syllogistic methods of argument, as he reigns to this day. His domi-

nance had, however, been challenged by Pierre de la Ramee, who perished at Paris in the Massacre of St. Bartholomew. Logicians were divided into contending schools of Ramists and anti-Ramists. Young Arminius not only expounded the innovating principles of Ramus but gave lessons in his own rooms on the subject.[1]

Arminius had undoubtedly been taught this form of logic at Marburg but found it extremely unpopular at Geneva. When it was banned there, he went for a time to the University of Basel. There he was so proficient that the faculty wished to confer upon him the Doctor of Divinity degree. Arminius declined this honor, feeling that he was too young and unworthy. The storm against him soon subsided, and Arminius returned to Geneva, where he stayed until 1586. After a short trip to Italy, he went back to Holland, where he was ordained as a minister of the Reformed Church in Amsterdam. He was a good pastor. Within a remarkably short time he was famous for his sermons, and the originality of his expositions of the Scriptures was greatly admired. Even at this very early stage, however, some were finding the breeding ground for heresy in his thought.

During Arminius' years as a pastor (1587-1603), the political and ecclesiastical situation was developing further. In spite of reverses—the worst of which had been the assassination of William the Silent in 1584—the Dutch were winning the war against Spain. The military genius of Maurice, the second son of William, had achieved such success that the Spanish no longer appeared in the northern provinces. This Protestant area had declared itself a republic at the outbreak of the rebellion and had found prosperity through shipping and trade. The merchants longed for

[1] Archibald H. W. Harrison, *The Beginnings of Arminianism* (London, 1926), p. 21.

peace, but the army chiefs and the lower classes of people first wanted to gain a decisive victory over the Spanish troops which were still entrenched all along the frontiers of the United Provinces, as the area had been called.

In the Reformed Church, Calvinism now prevailed. A presbyterian form of church government had been adopted. More and more the Belgic Confession and the Heidelberg Catechism had become the chief authorities next to the Bible. The history of the Belgic Confession is a remarkable one. Originally designed as an apology of the new Reformation faith addressed to King Philip of Spain, it had subsequently gained the position of a touchstone for orthodoxy. It had been written by Guy de Bray and was first printed in 1561. At a synod held at Antwerp in 1566, the Confession was modified, and from 1580 on there had been recurrent demands that it be subscribed to by the Reformed clergy. It is interesting that Calvin himself had always warned against putting any creedal statement on the same level as the Holy Scriptures. Indeed, in the beginning of the Reformation, it was the Lutherans who held to their Augsburg Confession more than the Calvinists to theirs. But later on, when Calvinism had reached a certain measure of consolidation, it was felt desirable to possess a sound symbol. In Holland, after so many years of uncertainty, it is understandable that many people wanted to be sure about the foundations of their faith. It was concerning the place of the Confession and the Catechism that Arminius began to make his voice heard.

There had already been some feeling that these formal statements ought to be checked against the Scriptures, since the Bible was the only ground upon which the Christian faith could be established. Arminius held this view, along with his friend Uitenbogaert, the influential court chaplain of Prince Maurice. They had been friends since student days in Geneva and now joined in wanting the Confession and the Catechism to be "revisable and reformable." But there was an additional motive behind this position—the desire for a solid front among Protestants.[2] It was their feeling that to adhere rigidly to one confession would be an obstacle to any and every attempt at union between churches of different orders.

Arminius' central idea—and this deserves frequent repetition—was that of a free church founded only upon the Holy Scriptures. During the days of his professorship at Leiden, he was to expound his opinions concerning a church where the Synod would "not assume to itself the authority of obtruding upon others, by force, those resolutions which may have been passed by unanimous consent." It was obvious to him that every member would agree, upon reflection, that it was possible for a synod to be both honest and in error. And then he quotes Tertullian who says: "Nothing is less a religious business than to employ coercion about religion." [3]

For Arminius, the state was obligated to maintain the opportunity for freedom of conscience. It must be admitted that it is difficult to follow the reasoning of Arminius and Uitenbogaert at this point. While the former was the greater theologian, the latter was the greater politician and possessed keen insight in

[2] James I and the Elector Palatine equally wanted to unite all Protestants against the threat of the Counter-Reformation. This accounts for a very interesting letter written by Arminius to Hyppolitus a Collibus, the personal representative of the Elector. It also accounts for their principle that to adhere rigidly to one confession would be an obstacle to any and every union between churches of different orders.

[3] *The Writings of James Arminius,* translated from Latin by James Nichols (Grand Rapids: Baker Book House, 1956), I, 189.

matters concerning the relation between church and state. It was Uitenbogaert who, upon the death of Arminius, drew up the "Remonstrance to the States of Holland," which in time produced the name "Remonstrants" in reference to the followers of Arminius. Uitenbogaert wanted to give the state more influence in church matters than we can appreciate today. Probably he feared an ecclesiastical hierarchy of Protestant ministers who would reign over the conscience and banish the idea of tolerance which had become so deeply rooted in Holland. In those days, after all, tolerance could be better protected by the governors of the state than by those of the church! Suffice it to say, however, that during the time Arminius was a minister at Amsterdam, quarrels continuously arose in the Dutch Reformed Church concerning the authority of creedal statements and questions of church order, and in these he was frequently involved.

Following his public exposition of the Epistle to the Romans, Arminius found himself confronted with charges of unorthodoxy. This was particularly true with regard to his statements about the seventh chapter of Romans. The problem for Arminius was Paul's statement, "I am carnal, sold under sin." Does the apostle, as Arminius puts it, "treat about a man who is still unregenerate, or about one who is already regenerate through the spirit of Christ?" The commonly accepted view ascribed Paul's words about the difficulty of following the law of God to the man to whom Christian salvation had come; this was simply a problem that would always be with the Christian. For Arminius, however, the words, "I am carnal, sold under sin," seemed to contradict Rom. 6:14, "Ye are not under law, but under grace." He felt that the prevalent view, in placing such limitations on the life of regenerate man, was seriously restricting the power of God.

Paul must be speaking of unregenerate man, said Arminius, for "the regenerate obtain the forgiveness of sins through faith in the blood of Jesus Christ and the power of his spirit." This same Spirit makes the Christian able to resist sin, gain a victory over it, and serve in "newness of life."[4] Arminius was unwilling to apply the words, "I am carnal, sold under sin," to the life of a believer.

This stance led to the accusation that Arminius was publicly proclaiming a position that had been declared heretical centuries before—Pelagianism.[5] Arminius defended himself by quoting both from the Fathers and from the more recent divines, the latter group including not only Bèze and Calvin but also Bruno, Erasmus, and Bucer. That he should quote theologians of the most divergent denominations and types—if he found truth in them—was typical. He even quoted Bellarmine, causing his adversaries to think him a Roman Catholic at heart. Called before an official body of his church, he was eventually cleared of the charges against him. This notwithstanding, it seems that Arminius did not have the proper feeling for the Lutheran paradox, *simul justus et peccator;* this is, that a man can be righteous and a sinner at one and the same time. Indeed, his distinction between unregenerate and regenerate man is far too rigorous.

In 1602 the plague struck the Netherlands. As a good pastor, Arminius called upon the sick without regard to personal danger. It is recorded that he behaved in a most courageous and truly Christian manner, indefatigably aiding and consoling many peo-

---

[4] *Ibid.,* II, 233.
[5] Pelagius was a British, or perhaps an Irish, monk who ascribed great importance to the freedom of the will. He held that after baptism man has full power and duty to keep the divine law.

ple all over the city of Amsterdam. At Leiden two professors of divinity succumbed, whereupon Arminius was immediately mentioned as the successor to one. Franciscus Junius the elder had been a very learned and respected man with whom Arminius had carried on a correspondence about predestination. Although not published until after his death, some of the letters from Arminius had been circulated, duplicates having been made in secret by one of Junius' students. The issue of predestination was to serve as the basis for an additional accusation of heresy against Arminius.

Many were opposed to the possible appointment of Arminius to a Leiden professorship. Among them was Franciscus Gomarus, who had been teaching exegesis and dogmatics at the University since 1594. He was a fervent Calvinist and taught supralapsarian predestination, the doctrine that before God created the world he decreed who should be saved and who should be damned, as opposed to infralapsarianism, the belief that this decision was not made until after the fall of Adam. At first Gomarus was squarely set against the idea of Arminius as a colleague, but after a long discussion between the two he was persuaded that on the main points they were in agreement. In 1603 the University conferred a doctor's degree upon Arminius. In his address on this occasion, he honored Gomarus as a "most illustrious man" and as his "very learned promoter." These good relations, however, were soon to be disturbed. The disturbance came the very next year, as a result of Arminius' lectures on predestination.

In the course of his lectures, he defined predestination as "the decree of the good pleasure of God in Christ, by which he resolved within himself from all eternity, to justify, adopt and endow with everlasting life, . . . believers on whom he had decreed to bestow faith." [6] It is evident that in this definition believers are the elect; in other words, faith precedes election. For Arminius, faith is not an effect of election, but is rather a necessary requisite in those who are to be elected. The decree concerning the bestowing of faith clearly precedes the decree of election. In fact, this is a paradox of the kind expressed by Paul in Phil. 2:12-13: "Work out your own salvation with fear and trembling; for God is at work in you, both to will and to work for his good pleasure" (R.S.V.). Arminius was to say to the States of Holland in 1608 that grace is "the commencement, the continuance and the consummation of all good." But grace, he added, is not irresistible, because "according to the scriptures, ... many persons resist the Holy Spirit and reject the grace that is offered." [7] He rejected supralapsarianism because he felt it made salvation by Jesus Christ merely a result of predestination. He would therefore repeat in his declaration to the States that this predestination "denies, that Christ is the meritorius cause, that again obtained for us the salvation which we had lost, by placing him as only a subordinate cause of that salvation which had been already foreordained, and thus only a minister and instrument to apply that salvation to us." [8]

Arminius also had a practical reason for rejecting supralapsarianism. He conceived of the love of God as being twofold—love of man and love of righteousness. For him, to believe only in God's love of men as sinners might well lead into a false security, a feeling that, in spite of men's sins, they will be saved by election in any case. To believe only in God's love of righteousness

---

[6] *Writings*, I, 565.
[7] *Ibid.*, pp. 253, 254.
[8] *Ibid.*, p. 230.

leads to despair, for men quickly learn that whatever they do to be righteous, perfection is still out of their reach. Thus Arminius held to the necessity of belief in the twofold love of God. In this way he sought to find a balance between the power of God's grace and the will of man, avoiding the extremes of supralapsarian predestination on the one hand and Pelagianism on the other. In his lectures at Leiden on this subject, however, he was laying the groundwork for a theological controversy that would have far-reaching consequences.

That same year, his colleague Gomarus decided to lecture on predestination also. He made it clear that he strongly opposed Arminius' views. Gomarus held that God saves some and damns others, "without any regard whatever to righteousness or sin, to obedience and disobedience, but purely of his own good pleasure to demonstrate the glory of his justice and mercy."

The reaction to the dissension between Arminius and Gomarus was immediate; their students were split into bitterly hostile camps. Soon the ministers of the Dutch Reformed Church were discussing the subject from the pulpit and making their congregations take sides in the conflict. It is difficult today to understand how an entire population can become so passionately involved in theological controversy, but it happened. Everywhere people discussed predestination. Families were divided and friends parted. Discussions took place in the market square, in the inn, and on board ship. Occasionally, after a sermon, some would go to the homes of friends of Arminius and provoke discord. Arminius himself was often insulted. It was even rumored that secretly he had forsaken the reformed faith during his brief visit to Italy in 1586. Representatives of the provincial synods came to Leiden seeking information about the dispute.

With these Arminius refused any discussion, hoping to present his position before an officially convened synod which would soon meet. The States General appointed a commission to arrange for a National Synod to consider the question. Both Arminius and Uitenbogaert were members, as well as several individuals who were open adversaries of Arminius, with the result that the commission could not agree. Would the synod be a free convention of the parties concerned, or would it be a court of justice, where a majority could lay down the law to a minority in matters of faith and conscience? In an oration on reconciling religious dissensions, Arminius had expressed the opinion in 1606 that a National Synod should be a free convention of Christians where everybody might speak according to his conscience and with the Scriptures as the only basis for truth. Among other things, he had declared:

May the God of truth and peace inspire the hearts of the magistrates, the people and the ministers of religion, with an ardent desire for truth and peace. May He exhibit before their eyes, in all its naked deformity, the execrable and polluting nature of dissension concerning religion; and may He affect their hearts with a serious sense of those evils which flow so copiously from it; that they may unite all their prayers, counsels, endeavors, and desires, and may direct them to one point, the removal of the causes of such a great evil, the adoption of a mild and sanatory process, and the application of gentle remedies for healing this dissension, which are the only description of medicines of which the very weak and sickly condition of the body of the Church, and the nature of the malady, may admit. "The God of Peace" who dignifies "the peace makers" alone with the ample title of "children," (Matt. V, 9,) has called us to the practice of peace.[9]

[9] *Writings, op. cit.,* I, 190.

This appeal had not been understood, and the strife had continued more fervently than ever. The adversaries of Arminius had even resorted to sending letters to foreign countries, accusing him of heresy. One such letter fell into the hands of Arminius and Uitenbogaert, convincing them not only of the possibility of personal harm but also of the threat to the reputation of Leiden University.

The controversy between Arminius and Gomarus became so serious that civil war seemed a lively possibility to some. Efforts were made to bring the men together and an invitation for them to appear before the States of Holland and expound their opinions was arranged. At first it seemed that there might be a chance to reconcile the two. Gomarus, however, publicly declared that:

The controversy between him [Arminius] and me, was of such immense importance, that, with the opinions which I professed, he durst not appear in the presence of his Maker, . . . that, unless some mode of prevention were promptly devised, the consequence would be, that the various Provinces, Churches and cities in his native land, and even the citizens themselves, would be placed in a state of mutual enmity and variance, and would rise up in arms against each other.[10]

After this statement, Arminius accepted the invitation to appear before the States of Holland and, accordingly, went before them on October 8, 1608, at The Hague. He had been preparing for some time for such a movement and was able to deliver a carefully developed "Declaration of Sentiments," in which he presented a complete exposition of his thought. This did not

[10] *Ibid.*, p. 194.

satisfy Gomarus. He also wanted to appear before the States to warn against the Pelagianism and Jesuitism of both Arminius and Uitenbogaert. Because the latter's influence in court circles was so pernicious, Gomarus particularly wanted to single him out for abuse. Before any additional statements to the States could be arranged, however, Arminius became seriously ill. He had gone to The Hague to make his second appearance, but was forced by his illness to return to Leiden, where he died on October 19, 1609.

It was said of Arminius that: "There lived a man in Holland who could be sufficiently esteemed only by those who knew him and who lacked esteem only in the eyes of those who knew him too little." Whenever he is commemorated, there is always the temptation to glorify him at the expense of his adversaries. Since to do this would be contrary to the spirit of Arminius himself, an objective appraisal of the man and his theology is in order.

It can be said in fairness that the opposition of Gomarus to Arminius was an attempt to keep reformed theology from succumbing to mere moralism. Supralapsarian predestination guards very well the idea of the absolute sovereignty of God, even though it is an outcome of Scholastic thinking. Arminius' opposition to it took him into the anti-Scholastic world which in turn led to the modern philosophy of the West and all the dangers of rationalism. He himself was no rationalist. His thought was fully informed by his faith, a faith based on the Bible and agreeing at nearly every point with the theology of the Fathers. Moreover, he was a Trinitarian. Never has he been shown to have had any connection with the theology of Socinus. On the contrary, he defended the Trinity in his *Disputations:* "He [God] is the First Person in the Sacred Trinity, who from all eternity of himself begat his Word, which is his Son, by communicating to Him his own Divinity." [11]

Arminius felt that Gomarus' doctrine of predestination was "repugnant to the nature of God, but particularly to those attributes of his nature by which he performs and manages all things, his wisdom, justice, and goodness." [12] He emphasized that whoever believes in Christ shall not perish, that God rewards "those that seek him." [13] This does seem to relegate faith to the area of works, but Arminius clearly explained in his disputation on free will that it is God's grace that makes faith possible.[14] Is this grace irresistible? If man cannot resist grace, he is but a puppet in God's hand. Arminius felt that "the controversy [about grace] does not relate to those actions or operations which may be ascribed to grace, but it relates solely to the mode of operation, whether it be irresistible or not." [15] In his opinion grace is resistible not because of its nature, but because of its mode of operation. God's love has allowed grace to be resisted because he does not want men to be puppets but to be children. Again and again Arminius quoted John 3:16: "For God so loved the world that he gave his only Son, that whoever believes in him should not perish but have eternal life." (R.S.V.) On the strength of Scripture, therefore, he maintained that a nonmechanical relationship exists between God and man.

It should be noted that it was not on the moral level that Arminius opposed supralapsarianism. Here he differed with Castellio, who has often been linked to him. They agreed in their

[11] *Ibid.*, p. 465.
[12] *Ibid.*, pp. 221-22.
[13] *Ibid.*, p. 234.
[14] *Ibid.*, p. 526.
[15] *Ibid.*, pp. 253-54.

plea for tolerance and in their views on predestination, but differed in their reasoning. And there was hardly any real relation between Arminius and the Dutch humanist Coornhert, although Arminius hesitated when commissioned by the Dutch Reformed Church to refute him. It seems obvious that, apart from the influence of the original Dutch Reformation that was connected with Melanchthon and Bullinger, much Calvinism can be found in the theology of Arminius; but he tried to be a Calvinist in a rather independent way. Such independence had existed in the early days of Calvinism, in men like Simon Grynaeus of Basel, Charles Perrot of Geneva, and to a certain extent, Junius of Leiden, writer of "The Peaceful Christian" and the man whom Arminius succeeded at the University. In the time in which Arminius lived, however, there was a tendency towards rigidity in Reformed discipline. This Arminius could not reconcile with his conscience. Therefore, there can be found in him a blending of the thinking of the first reformers and of those who heralded the coming of new times.

The theology of the Remonstrant Brotherhood has been characterized as *"Biblica, practica et irenica."* Although these words were written long after the death of Arminius, they express the essence of his theology. Fearing the dominance of subtle philosophical thinking over the truth of the gospel, he rooted his thinking in the Bible. And he tried to make his theology practical, leading to the worship of God. In his Inaugural Address he had declared:

For the theology which belongs to this world, is practical and through faith: Theoretical Theology belongs to the other world, and consists of pure and unclouded vision, according to the expression of the apostle, "We walk by faith, and not by sight;" (2 Cor. V, 7,). . . . For this reason, we must clothe the object of our theology in such a manner as may enable it to incline us to worship God, and fully to persuade and win us over to that practice.[16]

While he himself was peace-loving in both thought and behavior, it was Arminius' tragedy to have been incessantly involved in theological quarrels in spite of his personal feelings. It can only be hoped that a contemporary look at his life and struggle will make a contribution to a greater unity among Christian churches; nothing could be more fully in accord with his spirit.

[16] *Ibid.*, p. 60.

[2] From Arminius to Arminianism in Dutch Theology

Lambertus Jacobus van Holk *

There is a vast difference between the Arminius who lived in the seventeenth century and the Arminianism that exists today. Three hundred years of Christian thinking have produced not only a transformation in dogmatics, biblical studies, and discussions of the nature of the church, but also changes in the understanding of history itself. This transformation has come about chiefly through the quiet influence of books and ideas, although political and even military factors were also at work from time to time.

The developments within Arminianism after the death of its founder in 1609 bear unmistakable elements of historical irony. For one thing, the immediate consequence of Arminius' plea for a free, tolerant, national church was civil and ecclesiastical strife that led to the formation of a rigidly confessional church, with only a small, newly-founded denomination to insist on tolerance and freedom of conscience. Another unforeseen and ironical development was the increasing involvement of Arminianism in liberal theology and Dutch free

* This chapter has been rewritten for publication, and appears in this form by permission of the author.

Protestantism. As these changes are explored in some detail, it will become evident that, while open to new ideas and adaptable to rising occasions, Arminianism had adhered to its principle of a *via media*—not only between servitude and license in the matter of predestination but also between reactionary supernaturalism and revolutionary rationalism in later times.

In bridging the gap between Arminius and the Arminianism of today, the place to begin is the so-called Remonstrance of 1610, following his death the year before. A plea for moderation and Christian peace in the church, this document was drafted and signed by forty-four ministers of the Dutch Reformed Church and directed to the government of Holland. It indicated that these men were willing to take a moderate and reticent position in the controversy that had revolved around Arminius. With a view toward settling the theological disputes that were dividing the country, they sought official recognition of five points:

1) That those who believe in Christ are saved and those who do not are damned, and that neither is the result of divine predestination.

2) That Christ died on the cross for the redemption of all men, not just of the elect.

3) That man receives saving faith not from his own free will but from the grace of God by rebirth and renewal.

4) That all good works are solely due to the grace of God.

5) That although man can remain in a state of grace and will be sustained and protected by the Holy Spirit, it is possible for him, through his own negligence, to lose that state.

These statements of faith were the core of the theological battle that erupted in the years following Holland's war for independence from Spain. The battle ended with the Synod of Dort. Meeting in 1618 and 1619 this official body was widely representative of the Reformed churches, with delegates from Switzerland, Bremen, Hesse, The Palatinate, and England. It condemned Arminianism in strongly Calvinistic canons, reaffirming the Heidelberg Catechism and the Belgic Confession.

The synod excommunicated the followers of Arminius, who reacted almost immediately by assembling their loosely knit fellowship and founding the denomination that has since been known in church history as the Remonstrant Brotherhood. After some years of persecution and conflict, this new group settled into the general pattern of church life in the Netherlands. Perhaps bearing the trace of those years of trouble, its laws insisted repeatedly on the necessity of tolerance, peacefulness, and "knowledge of the truth which accords with godliness" (Tit. 1:1 R.S.V.). This was firmly within the limits of Arminius' own view that the unity and peace of the church were more important than theological controversy. Therefore, the organization of the Remonstrant Brotherhood could become a harbor of mild and practical Christianity, thereby showing itself to be the geniune child of Arminius' theology.

Throughout the seventeenth century there was in the Remonstrant movement little deviation from the central ideas of its founder. Two of its most illustrious leaders, Simon Episcopius (1583-1643) and Philip van Limborch (1633-1712), occupied the same general position as that seen at the beginning of the century. It is interesting to discover, however, that even within this continuity there appeared the first indications of discontinuity. Before the latter is discussed, a more systematic treatment of the developments within Remonstrant theology itself is in order. Five key areas merit consideration: (i) tolerance, (ii) biblical interpretation, (iii) the place of conscience in moral and religious matters, (iv) the influence of humanism and rationalism, and (v) universal grace.

As far as the area of tolerance is concerned, it must first be recognized that the word was widely used in both politics and theology during the seventeenth and eighteenth centuries. Taken up by the Enlightenment with strong conviction, its meaning ranged all the way from ill-disguised skepticism to the high virtues of lovingkindness and broadness of mind. It was in this Christian sense that the word was used in the Remonstrant Brotherhood. Combined with the ideal of freedom in matters of conscience, tolerance thus contributed to the concept of "the open church." When H. Y. Groenewegen indicated in his 1910 edition of the Remonstrance that the Arminian position could be summed up in the words anticlerical, anticonfessional, and antidogmatic, he was not far from the truth. These three terms have always characterized the Brotherhood and serve to explain why this small denomination did not become a closed sect, but rather remained a church open both to the world's needs and to its spiritual treasures.

There is more than latitudinarianism, however, in the ideal of tolerance. This exists in any truly national church, for no such church could ever succeed unless some degree of latitude would allow it to embrace within its fold different hues of opinion. Tolerance also implies malleability, as opposed to preciseness and rigidity. This aspect was so firmly rooted in the Dutch national character that Remonstrantism, after the short period of persecution, never again had to fight for its existence, as it was very much taken for granted. This was already true in the days of the Calvinistic United Provinces and was even more so after the French Revolution and in the era of constitutional monarchy. This is no mere gratuitous speculation but is rather written in the facts of history. The statement of church order given by King William I to the national church in 1816 is permeated by a spirit of tolerance that never ceased to vex the more Calvinistic groups within that church. Later in the nineteenth century the decree prescribing that ministers, presbyteries, and those to be confirmed as church members had to subscribe to the old formularies of faith merely "in spirit and in essentials" must be considered a kind of high-water mark in the influence of Arminian tolerance on the national church.

A second area meriting attention in a study of the development of Arminian theology is that of biblical interpretation. Arminius and his contemporaries were far closer to fundamentalism than is the present-day Remonstrant. When the Reformers put the Bible in the center of faith, worship, instruction, and ecclesiastical life, they did so in the firm, if naïve, belief that the Holy Scriptures interpreted themselves, since the Bible was clear and self-sufficient by virtue of its own content. In that belief, Luther and Calvin had always urged study of the text itself, implying that of Greek and Hebrew. No Latin translation such as the Vulgate, but fresh and painstakingly literal translations in the vernacular, straight from the original texts, would be the weapons to fight papal theology and Roman encroachments of tradition. They could not foresee the entirely different approach to the Bible that would be brought about by philological and historical research, a spreading knowledge of manuscripts and of the formation of the canon, and, above all, the deepening of insight into antique oriental civilization. These developments produced the idea of "exegesis from the mind of the author" (*exegesis e mente auctoris*), which came to be followed with presistence in linguistic and historical studies. The result was that the study of the Bible was gradually transformed into exactly the opposite of what was in the minds of the Reformers—and of Arminius. Here again the irony that so strongly marks the features of history is at work.

The type of thinking that conditioned the understanding of revelation in the Bible by its human origin and circumstances cannot be credited to Arminius himself, nor can he even be accused of favoring it. Yet it must be admitted that his careful, even cautious, attention to the real meaning of the Bible and his openness to the possibility of new truths hidden in its pages helped prepare the way for the new critical methods.

The wholehearted acceptance of the methods and results of scientific biblical study that took place within the Remonstrant Brotherhood does not mean that the practical authority of the Bible was rejected. If certain historical limitations and human deficiencies were felt more keenly than before, this should not imply a setting aside of the biblical message as such. In fact, critical research within the Brotherhood produced a fresh understanding of the Old Testament and its own particular religion. It also brought the value of the parables, and particularly the Sermon on the Mount, into sharpened focus.

These things notwithstanding, it still remains a far cry from Arminius' rather conservative, if objective, exegetical position to the views and methods of modern biblical interpretation.

A third area of interest in Arminianism, as it came to be understood in the Remonstrant Brotherhood, is the genuinely Protestant principle of the supremacy of the conscience in moral and religious matters. There is another echo of times of persecution in the basic article of church order among the Remonstrants, "That under no pretext may man be subjected to any compulsion in matters of conscience and religion." Even more than this, there is the implication of spiritual integrity here. In secular forms of organization, the supremacy of individual conscience has often produced disintegration. Within the Arminian fold, however, this tendency was balanced by the common aims of the members, the smallness of the denomination, and the pragmatic, pastoral emphasis of its religious life. Although this emphasis on the supremacy of the individual conscience was sometimes degraded as a moralistic reduction of the Christian faith, this criticism hardly did justice to the issue involved.

This feeling for the importance of the conscience and the need for personal conviction, leading to the use of persuasion rather than compulsion in all matters, had yet another important aspect—responsibility. Even if the popular view of freedom is to see it as freedom *from* any hampering ties one may feel, the deeper longing of every soul is freedom *for* its aims and ideals. This implies the willingness to accept responsibility, not only toward individual neighbors, but also toward the community as a whole. When Arminius pleaded for peace in the church and for solidarity among Christians of differing theological opinions, he was showing the same sense of responsibility that has motivated other leaders in the church to assume unpopular positions in difficult situations. While it is true that things have changed since 1600, the guiding spirit that has come to grips with these situations is the same in the modern Arminian as it was in Arminius.

Responsibility involves other tasks, such as the conscious development and social conditioning of the human personality, but this was not manifest at all in the seventeenth century. The Remonstrants of that day did not have the understanding of social issues that exists today, but they knew of the possibility of a pastoral attitude toward their neighbor, having discovered this in the pastoral letters of Paul, which they quoted extensively. Such an attitude was very much in the mind of Arminius as he insisted on peace and moderation. There can be no freedom for a man who is not prepared to admit that his brother has a right to it, too, on the common ground of the supremacy of the conscience.

A fourth area that must be considered in the development of Arminianism is the influence of humanism and rationalism. There was doubtless a connection between Arminianism and the thought of Erasmus (*ca.* 1466-1536), the Dutch humanist, whose concern was for ethical living and for peace in a Europe politically divided and troubled by recurrent wars. It is likely that the contributions of Erasmus came more through Episcopius, who succeeded Arminius at Leiden University, than through Arminius himself. As time went on, Arminian theology went farther and farther in the direction of a keen interest in humanistic learning and the philosophical interpretation of faith. The surest sign of this trend was the establishment of a professorship in philosophy at the Remonstrant seminary in Amsterdam in spite of the modest size and limited financial means of the denomination. This interest has gradually broadened into a very thorough reception of Western culture and participation in the secularization of European life. The modern Remonstrant is open toward the arts and sciences, toward historical developments, and toward society as a whole. It should be noted that this did not involve wholesale, uncritical acceptance of secularism. This openness to culture did not degenerate into mere identification with the world even during the nineteenth century, which saw an almost complete disappearance of the prophetic spirit. There are men of the prophetic voice today who find Remonstrants ready to listen to their efforts in restoring healthy, Christian church-consciousness to society.

The Arminian interest in secular culture has been not only a question of the prophetic versus the nonprophetic spirit, but also a grateful adaptation of cultural treasures to the religious life. Novels, poetry, and drama have had a great place in sermons, lectures, and religious instruction among the followers of Arminius. This development was facilitated as the "representative men" of Western culture were themselves imbued with Christian influences: Dante, Goethe, many nineteenth-century novelists, and men like Shakespeare who by their realistic portrayals of human character helped man interpret himself. This synthesis becomes increasingly difficult with the clearly antireligious writers of today. On the other hand, Remonstrants happily acknowledge the trend of modern church architecture, developing since

1900-20, which proves that art and religion can still be inspiring to each other.

The last and more strictly religious characteristic of Arminian theology that needs to be mentioned is the doctrine of universal grace as it is illustrated by the text of I John 2:2: "And he [Jesus Christ, the righteous] is the expiation for our sins, and not for ours only but also for the sins of the whole world" (R.S.V). Origen's idea of universal grace, indicating that ultimately all who had fallen away from God would be restored to full harmony with him, had been condemned by the church as being heretical. When they quoted the words of First John, Arminius and the early Remonstrants certainly had no such sweeping concept as this is mind; they were, in keeping with their mildness of temperament, opposing the dark violence of Calvin's predestination. Perhaps they were also concerned about the dangerous Pharisaism of minorities who considered themselves as the elect. At any rate, they were happy to find the biblical confirmation for their belief that was provided by First John. There is indeed a temperamental affinity between Arminius and his doctrine. Fortunately, there are Christians in every age whose eternal felicity is not increased by the smell of the reprobate burning in hellfire; they can neither understand nor accept for themselves any happiness that is not shared by others—no, by *all* others!

This temperamental mildness is very closely related to divine love. Although all love is probably more or less gratuitous and unmerited, divine love by its very nature is profoundly inclusive and creative in its activity of maintaining, restoring, and saving the world. Nothing shows the depth of God's love more thoroughly than the propitiatory sacrifice of Christ; the more we attribute to him and the greater the price of his death, the farther this sacrifice extends into all spheres of life, both cosmic and human. While we mortals may grant justice to all and grace but to a few, the intensity of compassion and the inherent nature of God's love do not know such a restriction. In its indication of the mystery of divine love, the doctrine of universal grace is emphatically evangelical. If we agree that Anselm of Canterbury was right in saying, "Thou hast not yet pondered deeply enough on the gravity of sin," we should answer with all due reverence, "Thy saintly spirit, Sir, has not yet pondered enough on the power of love." Such firm mildness, to be sure, would be perfectly in accord with the thought of Arminius.

It cannot be said that this doctrine of universal grace is often preached by Remonstrants, although it fits in very well with their ideas of tolerance, practical Christianity, and pastoral concern. This is probably the result of taking the doctrine for granted, which has become easier as the opposite presupposition of eternal punishment in a real hell has largely lost ground among modern man.

It must also be noted that such concepts as "all the world" and "propitiatory sacrifice" acquired a different meaning as scholars began to objectively study non-Christian religions instead of merely belittling the heathen. It was a Remonstrant of the nineteenth century who founded the discipline of comparative religion in the Netherlands. Giving the other world faiths a share in God's truth, and thereby in salvation, implied a practice of *conferring* rather than of *converting*. The initial urge of the missionary enterprise weakened, but has reawakened in this century as a result of developments in many areas. This revival of interest is not surprising in these times when the Christian faith is more and more immediately confronted with the issue of the value and truth of the non-Christian religions in a world rapidly moving toward some form of coexistence. All this, however, is far afield of Arminius himself, who would have been no more ready for so wide an application of the doctrine of universal grace than were his contemporaries. It may well be that Christianity will have to make the belief in universal grace central if it is to have any chance of meeting and being met by other world religions in a spirit of good will and a readiness to listen.

Now, considering the five areas mentioned above in the development of Arminianism, it can clearly be seen that its theology has been on the move in a fascinating interplay of continuity and discontinuity with Arminius' own position. The diversity of conviction thus exposed has not been merely relative but has resulted from a deep feeling of the need for confession and belonging together, even to the extent of accepting the fact of brotherhood among adversaries. Arminian theology, by its very origin and by its permanent structure, has indeed been an anchorage for the hope of eventual human unity through its generous belief in God as the Father of all races and classes and in the freedom and responsibility of man in and through Jesus Christ.

There are some additional influences and trends that must be understood in the transition from Arminius to Arminianism in Dutch theology.

For one thing, there was the impact of Descartes in the second half of the seventeenth century. Hotly opposed by the Calvinists, his ideas were welcomed among the Remonstrants. Two professors in the seminary at Amsterdam, Stephanus Curcellaeus and Jean Le Clerc, educated the future ministers of their day in accordance with the principles of rational insight, which was far from common then. In his contribution to the commemorative study during the tercentenary celebration of the seminary in 1934, G. J. Sirks suggests that the desire to preserve the intellectual and moral integrity of the human personality led these men to follow Descartes. Here was a new beginning, for Descartes represented the dawn of modern Western philosophy. Curcellaeus and even the more conservative Limborch felt that it was only by relating revelation and reason that a workable theology could be formulated that would be abreast of the problems of a new era. There was constant correspondence between Remonstrant theologians and the secular thinkers of their day. It was not only Descartes who held their interest; so did John Locke. Both Limborch and Le Clerc befriended him during the time he was an exile from his own country. This was a prelude to the relationships of the eighteenth-century Enlightenment, and it surpassed the sometimes pedestrian level of this later movement by the injection of a simple but steadfast Christian devotion. Moreover, there were contacts during this period between Dutch Arminians and English Platonists. Rosalie L. Colie investigated this in her well-known book, *Light and Enlightenment,* and summarizes her research in these words:

> Arminianism was in the beginning the result of the common-sense, humanistic attitude towards religion, metaphysics, physics, and human society, attractive to men of good will in England as in Holland: it gave authority to Mede, Whichcote, More, Cudworth and their fellows; it took in its turn much from their philosophic idealism. . . . [so that] the Arminian and Platonist traditions become inextricably mingled to exert a force upon European thinking.[1]

[1] (New York: Cambridge University Press, 1957), p. 144.

If this pattern is not exactly Arminius, it still moves along the *via media* of disciplined Christian freedom.

In a drama more or less similar to that in which Curcellaeus and Le Clerc participated, the two Swiss refugees J. J. Wetstein and Daniel Albert Wyttenbach taught at the Remonstrant seminary in the eighteenth century. There was a great deal of discussion about these men and their reputation of being heretical in their opinions. It must be remembered that the pre-1789 Dutch Republic was not entirely tolerant. Yet, Wetstein could publish his careful, critical edition of the New Testament and Wyttenbach could teach his beloved classical authors, especially Cicero.

If both of these men were continuing the tradition that had been fostered ever since the Renaissance, a much more up-to-date enterprise came in the work of Paulus van Hemert. Also a professor at the seminary, he was the first to introduce into the Netherlands the philosophy of Immanuel Kant. It would be a long time before the abstruse speculations of Kant's transcendental thinking were absorbed by the Dutch, accustomed as they were to the matter of fact and utilitarian ways of the Enlightenment. Addressing himself to a people inclined by nature to solid, commonsense philosophy and realism, Hemert's introduction was almost in vain; a real appreciation of Kant had to wait until well into the nineteenth century. The significant thing about this whole situation was that the seminary offered Hemert the possibility of teaching unusual ideas.

During the much praised and blamed nineteenth century, Arminian attitudes became more widespread. This was the heyday of liberalism, and, in many respects, the borderline between it and Arminianism became obscured. The Remonstrant Brotherhood did not immediately adopt "modernism." It wasn't until late in that century (1872-73) that the decision was made to transfer the seminary from Amsterdam to Leiden, then the bulwark of modernism. By this symbolic deed, the Remonstrants made it clear to everybody that they thought their real place was in modernism. Long before this, however, the principles of freedom, tolerance, ethical living, broad-mindedness, and criticism had found increasing reception everywhere: in the laity of the Dutch Reformed Church, in theological faculties, and among the leading men of social life and politics.

The figure of one man needs to be presented at this point—Jan Hendrik Scholten, the "grand old man" of modernism. His *magnum opus* was entitled *The Doctrine of the Dutch Reformed Church*. The basis for this doctrinal system, according to Scholten, was God's absolute sovereignty and his free grace. Although this sounds like orthodoxy, the book itself was attacked by conservative groups as leaning dangerously toward heresy. While he felt that the *formal* principle of Dutch Reformed theology was freedom of the will (he boldly characterized the religion of the New Testament as "the religion of freedom"), he energetically defended what he considered to be the *material* principle—God's sovereignty and free grace—against all comers, even against Arminius and the Remonstrance of 1610. His contention was that predestination was thought of in too mechanical a fashion. Scholten did not keep up with the times; Arminianism had already been permeated by the stress on human activity, the concern with the historical background of the Bible, and the demands of freedom for research and freedom from creeds and dogma. The spirit of the Remonstrance, in fact, was setting the pace for liberalism.

The nineteenth century saw an increasing difficulty in differentiating between these two terms. The new location of the seminary at Leiden had something to do with this process. There Remonstrant ministers-to-be were subjected to Cornelius Petrus Tiele's views on comparative religion, Abraham Kuenen's method of teaching the Old Testament, Johannes G. R. Acquoy's lectures on church history, and Scholten's New Testament exegesis, along with that of his successor, Manen, who was also of a liberal bent. Remonstrants early began to participate in various forms of liberal church work, such as annual meetings of representatives from various theological traditions, co-operative youth movements, and efforts in mass communication.

To this very day, the Remonstrant Brotherhood is the only basically nonconfessional denomination in the Netherlands; and here another example of the irony of history must be mentioned—that a church so oriented could also support the more evangelical trend that turned the tide of nineteenth-century liberalism. The present century has witnessed a new comprehension of several elements of Christian tradition—the tension between the transcendence and the immanence of God, the experience of human sin and guilt and that of saving grace and redemption, together with a new understanding of the Person of Christ. Arminian thinking is presently showing itself to be as independent as ever by its readiness to revive the more specifically evangelical values without feeling the pressing need of the Barthian cure which some other groups have considered so urgent.

Along with this renewal of interest in the inner religious life, there has been a renewed understanding of the importance of community. This is a rather complex issue. On the one hand, there is the undeniable trend toward the organization of religious activities through central denominational leadership and interchurch co-operation. This the Arminians need. There has been, however, in recent years the development of an institutionalism that is clearly alien to the Arminian tradition. It has been a kind of evangelical High-Church trend that will find little acceptance in a group that, in matters of ecclesiastical policy, is decidedly Low Church. This position has been the result not so much of a closely guarded but obsolete individualism as it has of an evangelical diffidence toward institutionalism as such. Time and again, Christianity has accepted the load of this all-too-human institutionalism in church affairs, with its concomitant use of expediency and inevitably sly methods of diplomacy, just as soon as a denomination becomes important enough to make its voice heard over the world. The Remonstrant Brotherhood is on its guard against this, for it is always dangerous to the purity of the Christian life for a church to be persuaded to use unholy means for holy ends, particularly when the clergy have the tendency to condone this. Another reason for attempting to preserve the spiritual interpretation of the religious community is that the church, as a free association, is one of the last strongholds for the integrity of the human personality in a world that is increasingly being influenced by collectivism, technocracy, and cybernetics. The Remonstrant Brotherhood, guided by Arminian theology, may well be considered as a refuge for the soul.

For the information of those outside Holland, the latest trend in that theology—the effort for renewal by increased concentration on the doctrine of the Holy Spirit—needs to be briefly sketched. There is very little that is astonishing about this, for Arminians have always put the vivifying spirit before the letter of the law, in accordance with Paul. Remonstrants have always asked that theories be tested in practice by a life that is inspired, guided, and comforted by the Holy Spirit. It seems to many of the leaders of the Brotherhood that a fresh interpretation of this doctrine is in order, and some writing on this subject has already appeared. This doctrine is related both to Christian tradition and modern universal demands, to spontaneous testimony, personal experience, and to control by Scripture. It also speaks adequately of both the personal and the social aspect of guidance. A balance is being sought between rigid institutionalism and mere fluid and transient emotionalism. This latest trend is still in its beginning, but there is confidence that here is fresh fruit ripening on the venerable tree of Arminianism and a promising variation of that ancient *via media* that will lead to a future in which the best of Arminius' heritage can be applied to the needs and tasks of the then-living theologians and congregations. Such a future is not certain, but there is hope that Arminian theology will inspire the completion of a double task—the providing of breadth and depth to both ecumenical work and the existential enterprise of guiding mankind toward true peace and unity through the old Arminian principle that theology should be biblical, practical, and irenical. If this double task is realized, it might well be said that Arminius, although no Arminian himself, prepared the way for Arminianism.

In conclusion, let those who feel inspired by the spirit of Arminius share the rich inheritance that has come through him by repeated investigations of his theology and the unity and diversity of Arminianism. As these studies are made, it would seem that the following aspects would merit special attention:

1) The belief in the universal grace of God as it has been revealed in the gospel of Jesus Christ as the common basis of all men. This encourages Christians in the missionary spirit inherent in the gospel, as they acknowledge the share in truth and salvation that belongs to non-Christian religions as a result of this universal grace.

2) The persuasion that, in discussing the scope of Christian freedom, emphasis should be placed upon present personal and social responsibility rather than upon the predestinational controversy as such. If this is done, the grace of God and the freedom of man do not seem to be two separate items, but are rather understood as two integral parts of a permanent dialogue.

3) The belief that Arminius' plea for peace, moderation, and love in the church is by no means antiquated but is needed now more than ever before on the national, racial, and class levels.

4) The feeling that the study and exegesis of the Bible should be as impartial and objective as possible, using the best methods available. This will provide for the development of a dynamic, prophetic dialogue between the church and the world.

5) The emulation of Arminius' open-minded appreciation of ancient civilizations. This will insure a similarly open-minded awareness of both the treasures and failures of all cultures, regardless of their age or their nature.

[3] The Influence of Arminianism in England

Geoffrey F. Nuttall

I am inclined to begin by recounting two recent incidents which together may serve as an interesting pointer. Among the papers required for a higher degree in one of the English universities is an essay with three or four alternative subjects, and one of these subjects a few years ago, I remember, was: "Since Wesley we are all Arminians." One of the alternatives that year was an invitation to discuss the dictum, "Thou shalt not suffer a witch to live"—so we need not assume that the assertion that Arminianism is now universally accepted was regarded as indisputable! It is interesting, nonetheless, that the assertion could be made.

The other incident happened more recently. I was speaking of this Arminius Symposium to a friend who, though not a minister, has written one or two books on subjects relating to Wesleyan Methodism; and I received the answer, "Do you know, I never realized that there was anyone called Arminius!" In part, no doubt, this reflects the contented ignorance of theology common among Englishmen, but to a shrewd observer it may suggest the genuine triumph of Arminianism. In the last decades there has been a revival of Calvinism in Europe, but a revival of Arminianism is difficult to imagine. "Since Wesley we are all

Arminians" whether we know it or not, whether we have ever heard of Arminius or not. Arminius has triumphed much as, in a far shorter time, Sigmund Freud has triumphed; all of us think differently because of Freud, even those who have never heard of him.

"The influence of Arminianism in England" is a vast subject. "How interesting!" said a clergyman of the Church of England to me; "Launcelot Andrews and Archbishop Laud and all those people in their struggles with the Puritans in the seventeenth century!" Truly, the doctrinal transformation of the Church of England in the generation between the Synod of Dort and the death of Laud would amply repay a paper on its own account. The oft-repeated *bon mot* in reply to the question, "What do the Arminians hold?" namely, "The best bishoprics and deaneries in all England," was by no means devoid of truth; it is a pity, however, if the witticism diverts attention from a change of sentiment which raised genuine theological issues as well as social, political, and financial—not to mention the philosophical issues so attractively prosecuted in Colie's recent study, *Light and Enlightenment*.

"The influence of Arminianism in England." "How interesting!" said another friend to me. He is a Unitarian, and he thought of the subject as connoting the dawn of the light of reason in religion; the light which, as the eighteenth century proceeded, would break out into bright sunshine in Arianism and Socinianism.

Any English Methodist regards Arminianism as his own communion's peculiar preserve—and not unjustly. Did not the Methodists institute in 1778 a periodical with the brave title *The Arminian Magazine: Consisting of Extracts and Original Trea-*

tises on Universal Redemption? Even in 1778, apparently, an Arminian could regard the Battle of the Decrees as won. "Whatsoever was the case in times past," writes the editor, John Wesley, in the first number, "very few now receive them (the Decrees) even in Holland. And in Geneva they are universally rejected with the utmost horror. The case is nearly the same in England." In 1778 Arminius' name was still in use, as a bogey; it was not much more. "We know nothing more proper to introduce a work of this kind," Wesley continues, "than a sketch of the Life and Death of Arminius: a person, with whom those who mention his name with the utmost indignity, are commonly quite unacquainted; of whom they know no more than of Hermes Trismegistus."[1] It is fair to observe that after only one generation the commemoration of Arminius gave place to an eponymous title; in 1805 *The Arminian Magazine* became *The Methodist Magazine.*

Then there were the Quakers, who in the pages of history precede the Methodists by almost a hundred years. They seem always to have been universalists. "Arminians without Arminius" one might venture to term them, remembering their noted abhorrence of all "notions," as they called theology. They would then offer an inviting avenue for exploration in the search for the *anima naturaliter Arminiana* in a century when so little is allowed to be natural. In fact, however, the first Quakers were not wholly in ignorance of Arminius. They were not allowed to be by the writers who controverted their universalism. One of the largest and most effective defenses of early Quakerism is to be found in a treatise published in 1660 by Samuel Fisher, the subject of a recent dissertation by Edna Hall.

---

[1] *The Arminian Magazine* (London), I, viii, v.

Samuel Fisher had begun his career as a clergyman of the Church of England, and before this he had enjoyed a university education; so it was somewhat ironically that he entitled his book *Rusticus ad Academicos*. It takes the form of a reply to attacks on Quakerism by four eminent contemporaries—Richard Baxter, John Owen, John Tombes, and Thomas Danson. "These Four," Fisher says, "do as one man withstand and resist this Truth the Qua:(kers) testifie, concerning the general love and Grace of God in Christ Jesus to all mankind, i.e. every individual man." "Arminiana sunt omnia jamdudum profligata," "they are all Arminius his matters (quoth J.O.), Arminian points (quoth T.D.), thus they stun men's minds; not knowing," Fisher adds with alliterative emotion, "that Arminius (though deem'd and doom'd an Heretick by that Divine and domineering denunciation of the Divines at Dordt) was as no less learned, so fully as holy and honest as themselves." [2]

But it is not only in the variegated life of those denominations which makes the story of English Protestantism such a multicolored picture that the subject, "The influence of Arminianism in England," is vast. If at all adequately dealt with, it would include, besides the gradual, and eventually almost insensible, adoption of the doctrine of general redemption, the consideration of the increasingly large place allowed to reason in religon as over against superstition; also it would show the growth in mutual tolerance among Christians and the toleration of multiformity in religion by the State, which came to accompany this. All these phenomena undoubtedly had other theological, and also other more secular, contributory causes besides what may, broadly speaking, be called Arminianism; but Arminianism played no

[2] (London: 1660), IV, 83-84.

small part. In the English scene in the seventeenth century the cause of religious liberty owed much, undeniably, to the Independents; but "it is a natural conjecture," as Douglas Nobbs has written, "that the Independents were directly inspired by Remonstrant principles, particularly as (Philip) Nye developed theories closely related to the argument of Episcopius," who "valued the liberty of sects as a moral pearl of great price."[3]

Self-confessed Arminianism in England is to be found, in the main, in one or the other of two contrasting movements. One of these two movements leads on into Arianism, Socinianism, and Unitarianism and eventually decreases in numbers and influence. The other remains Trinitarian and Evangelical and increases. Why is this so? It is largely from within the confines of this question that we shall regard the subject. The answer, if we can find one, should be illuminating.

First, let me illustrate the way things went in the eighteenth century when Arminian tenets were adopted in churches which already existed, and let me do so from the situation in Wales. The history of religion in Wales has its differences from the history of religion in England, but at this point the story is one and the same; and the area of the principality is sufficiently small and compact to allow a reasonably comprehensive but brief survey.

The first great name here is that of Jenkin Jones, an Independent who—it is interesting to note—appears under the heading "Arminian minister" in the *Dictionary of Welsh Biography* published last year by the Honourable Society of Cymmrodorion,

---

[3] Douglas Nobbs, *Theocracy and Toleration* (New York: Cambridge University Press, 1938), pp. 103, 105.

where he is described as "the apostle of Arminianism."[4] Jenkin Jones began to preach the new doctrines in opposition to the Calvinism traditional among the Independents in 1726. In 1733 he built a meetinghouse at Llwynrhydowen in Cardiganshire, "the first Arminian chapel in Wales." After his death in 1742 he was succeeded in the pastorate by his nephew, David Lloyd. Now David Lloyd, who died in 1779, was apparently an Arian—his assistant and successor, David Davis, certainly was so. Another generation passed and Arianism began to give way to Unitarianism. In 1802 David Lloyd's son Charles, who had declared himself a Unitarian, led a secession of sympathizers from Llwynrhydowen to found two distinct Unitarian churches. This is regarded as "the official beginning of Unitarianism in Cardiganshire," and thus in Wales as a whole. David Davis, who continued at Llwynrhydowen, remained an Arian, but after his retirement in 1820 the church proved unable to stand against the new trend. His successor in the pastorate, John Davies, was a Unitarian; and today Llwynrhydowen is regarded as the mother church of Unitarianism in Wales.

A similar development may be watched elsewhere in the principality. At Cwm-y-glo, Merthyr Tydvil, in Glamorganshire, the first minister to preach Arminian tenets was Roger Williams. In 1730 he died, and his assistant and successor, James Davies, remained a Calvinist. But the minister chosen to assist Davies, Richard Rees, was an Arminian. In 1747 Rees led a secession from Cwm-y-glo to form a new church at Cefncoedcymer. This church, like Llwynrhydowen, has long since been Unitarian. In 1787 the

[4] Sir John Lloyd and R. T. Jenkins, eds. *Dictionary of Welsh Biography* (Oxford, Eng.: B. H. Blackwell, Ltd., 1959). For the English reader this *Dictionary* provides a convenient account of Arminianism in Wales. See the articles on the ministers mentioned in the following paragraphs.

same thing took place at Glandŵr in Pembrokeshire. Seventeen members were excommunicated for Arminianism and formed a new church across the county border in Carmarthenshire at Rhydyparc. This church likewise in time became Arian, and by 1848 its minister was a Unitarian.

Llwynrhydowen, Cwm-y-glo, and Glandŵr were all Independent churches. Arminian tenets also appeared at much the same time among the Baptists in Wales who—like the Independents—were traditionally Calvinist. In 1749 Charles Winter, the assistant minister of the church at Hengoed in Glamorganshire, was excommunicated for Arminianism, and with twenty-three sympathizers formed a new church at Craig-y-fargod. By 1792 the minister of Craig-y-fargod, Daniel Isaac, had become a Unitarian. He resigned, but by 1809 the church itself had become Unitarian.

In 1790 Craig-y-fargod was still the only Arminian Baptist Church in the principality.[5] But nine years later a fresh wave of Arminianism broke over the Welsh Baptists, and a number of churches seceded on these grounds. The sequel here is interesting. By this time Evangelical Arminianism, in the form of Wesleyan Methodism, was belatedly making itself felt in Wales. Those Arminian Baptist churches whose ministers welcomed the Wesleyans were rejoining before long their former co-religionists, the Calvinist or Particular Baptists. The other Arminian Baptist churches, only three of which are still in existence, Wick and Nottage in Glamorganshire, and Pant Teg in Carmarthenshire, eventually, like Craig-y-fargod, became Unitarian.[6]

[5] Joshua Thomas, *History of the Baptist Association in Wales* (London: 1795), p. 55.
[6] Lloyd and Jenkins, *op. cit.* See entries under James Davies (ca. 1767-1860), Evan Lloyd (1764-1847), Benjamin Phillips (1750-1839), William Thomas (d. 1813), Moses Williams (d. 1810).

In England—as is well known—the same steady movement of those Dissenters who had espoused Arminian tenets towards Arianism and Socinianism took place throughout the eighteenth century. In England the movement affected not so much the Independent and Baptist as the Presbyterian churches; till by 1844, when the present Presbyterian Church of England began to rise from the older English Presbyterian churches which still existed, scarcely one had not become Unitarian. Why, the question is, did this development not likewise affect the Methodist Societies which arose in much the same period, since these were equally insistent in their proclamation of Arminianism? By and large Methodism, while remaining unashamedly Arminian, has also continued Trinitarian. It is true that in 1817 there was a small secession in Lancashire, the supporters of which took the title of Methodist Unitarians. But they never spread beyond the district of their origin and they can hardly be said to possess much significance for historical theology (though they may for the history of Chartism).[7]

Let us ask another question. Whence and why did the Methodist Societies adopt Arminianism? Perhaps this question is too large. Whence, then, and why did Wesley adopt Arminianism? Possible answers to these questions are many, but I propose to suggest three.

The first is that Wesley was born and grew up in a favorable area; Arminianism was in the air he breathed. Lincolnshire was a stronghold of Arminianism in England almost a century before the new doctrine reached Wales. To begin with, the first English

---

[7] Herbert McLachlan, *The Methodist Unitarian Movement* (Manchester: The University Press, 1919).

Baptist, John Smyth, who also became the first English General or Arminian Baptist, was from the Lincolnshire town of Gainsborough, not far from Wesley's birthplace. True, Smyth did not become an Arminian until after he had moved to the Netherlands in 1608, but his influence may have continued among those whom he left behind him or may have been restored by some of his companions in exile who returned home. This is conjecture, but by 1651 the Arminian Baptist movement in Lincolnshire was sufficiently conscious, organized, and vocal for it to supply twelve out of the thirty churches in eight English Midland counties which in that year issued a joint *Faith and Practise,* and by 1673 there were as many as thirty-three centers in the county.[8] The part of Lincolnshire called the Isle of Axholme, of which Epworth—Wesley's birthplace and early home—is the capital, was particularly Arminian. In 1669 it was reported to the Bishop of Lincoln that the General Baptist conventicle in the parish of Epworth numbered fifty-seven supporters, a further fifty-seven were reported at Belton, thirty-four at Crowle, and twenty-four at Haxey. These villages—three of the six parishes which with Epworth make up the Isle—also are mentioned in the record of the General Baptist Church at Epworth. In 1673 the church members numbered 126.[9] Their minister, John Norfolk, had in 1661 been among the signatories to a *Humble Address from Lincoln* to Charles II.[10] In 1699 the church enclosed a piece of

---

[8] William Thomas Whitley, ed., *Minutes of the General Assembly of the General Baptist Churches in England* (1909), I, lxii-lxiii.

[9] A. de M. Chesterman, *Axholme Baptists* (Crowle, Lincolnshire: 1949), pp. 15, 20. There is a copy of this pamphlet in Dr. Williams' library, London.

[10] Whitley, *op. cit.,* p. xl.

land as a burial ground—always a sign of virility in English Dissent.[11] This was four years before John Wesley's birth.

The strength of Arminianism in the district may be attributed in part to the fact that during the reign of Charles I 60,000 acres of the surrounding swamps (which gave the Isle of Axholme its name) had been drained by Dutchmen under the supervision of Cornelius Vermuyden, and that in course of time some two hundred Dutch families had settled here.[12] It is not surprising that some of these were among the Dissenters reported to the bishop in 1676.[13] Wesley's father Samuel Wesley, the rector of Epworth, probably had no love for these Baptists among his parishioners, who in general gave him frequent trouble. Samuel Wesley's biographer, writing a hundred years ago, describes the inhabitants of Epworth as "little better than Christian savages"; although two pages later he quotes an account of them written in 1821 as "good-natured, simple, sincere, humble, and singularly modest."[14] Whatever doubt may exist concerning their character, there is none concerning the doctrine of a number of them. It is at least suggestive that the greatest English Arminian was reared in a village and neighborhood to which active and self-confessed Arminianism had long been no stranger.

It may be convenient here to conclude the story of these English General Baptists. Like the church at Craig-y-fargod in Wales, their churches later turned in the main to Arianism and Socinianism. In 1770 a number of churches which deplored this

---

[11] Adam Taylor, *History of the English General Baptists* (London: 1818), II, 425-26.
[12] L. Tyerman, *Life and Times of the Rev. Samuel Wesley, M.A.* (London: Simpkin, Marshall & Co., 1866), p. 332.
[13] Chesterman, *op. cit.*, p. 15.
[14] Tyerman, *op. cit.*, pp. 331, 333.

development formed a separate General Baptist New Connexion. This New Connexion, as a recent Baptist historian remarks, "was obviously a child of the Methodist Revival "[15] as its founder, Dan Taylor, and others of its originators had come under Methodist influence. In 1815 the church at Epworth joined the New Connexion; this also was under local Methodist influence.[16] Like the General Baptist Churches in Wales which welcomed the coming of Wesleyan Methodism, the churches of the New Connexion were later absorbed among the Calvinistic or Particular Baptists. The final official amalgamation between the two bodies into the present Baptist Union of Great Britain and Ireland took place in 1891, and distinctions of origin are now forgotten.[17] The Socinianizing General Baptist churches, on the other hand, are now, in every case where they still exist, Unitarian. Their General Assembly, which first met in 1660, still exists as a legal entity and meets annually, but it is now only a shadow of its former self. It includes only eleven churches in England and two of the three churches in Wales mentioned earlier. The third one and one or two churches in England of General Baptist origin do not send representatives to the Assembly.[18]

Let us return to Wesley. There was indeed no need for him to go to his Baptist neighbors to learn Arminianism. He learned it at home from his parents. As good Anglicans, the rector of Epworth and his wife were of course Arminians. Of course, but

---

[15] Alfred Clair Underwood, *History of the English Baptists* (London: Carey Kingsgate Press, 1947), p. 153.
[16] Taylor, *op. cit.*, p. 427.
[17] Underwood, *op. cit.*, p. 216.
[18] These statistics were obtained from the late Rev. Wilfred Waddington, Secretary of the General Assembly of the General Baptists, and Jeremy Goring.

not as a matter of course. Both Wesley's parents were remarkable people, his mother no less than his father. Each of them had grown up in Calvinistic Dissent in a family which had braved suffering for conscience' sake. For both of them Arminianism was a position fought through to, when, independently of each other, they had abandoned the influence of home and ancestry for the Established Church. Wesley's father "fearlessly repudiates the doctrines of election and reprobation" in more than one of his published pieces.[19] In the first number of *The Arminian Magazine* Wesley printed a "Hymn to the Creator" by his father, which includes the lines:

> No Evil can from Thee proceed:
> 'Tis only suffer'd, not decreed.[20]

In 1725 when Wesley was just twenty-two, his mother Susannah Wesley, wrote to him thus: "The Doctrine of Predestination, as maintained by rigid Calvinists, is very shocking, and ought utterly to be abhorred; because it charges the most holy God with being the Author of Sin." This letter Wesley also printed in the first number of *The Arminian Magazine*.[21] It continues with what John Newton, in a recent prize essay on Susannah Wesley, justly calls "an exposition of Rom. 8:29 f which breathes the authentic evangelical Arminianism which was of the essence of her son's developed theology." Whether or not it owed anything to the ambient air of Lincolnshire, Wesley's Arminianism—as well as much else in Methodism—certainly owed a good deal to his parents.

[19] Tyerman, *op. cit.*, p. 144.
[20] P. 44.
[21] P. 37.

From his parents, indeed, Wesley not only learned Arminian doctrine directly; he learned something else, which at the time was far rarer and more remarkable, and which, it may be argued, profoundly affected his Arminianism and his reasons for holding to it so firmly. This was a missionary outlook. To quote his father's biographer: "The missionary spirit was a passion in the Wesley family, when Christian missions to the heathen scarce existed." [22] This may sound exaggerated, but solid grounds for the statement may be adduced. The first Church of England missionary society called the Society for Propagating the Gospel in Foreign Parts was founded in 1701. Its original interests, however, were confined to those parts of the world where English colonies and plantations were to be found. In 1705 Wesley's father not only "suggested a scheme for the conversion of Jews, Mohammedans and heathens," [23] but offered to go himself as a missionary to Abyssinia, India, or China for the sake of the heathen whose language he expressed himself willing to learn, as well as to any of the English colonies or to any existing native churches.[24]

One may wonder how far this desire Samuel Wesley had conceived was shared by his wife. At the time she was probably more concerned with his improvidence and imprisonment for debt. Later when her son "expressed a wish to preach to the North American Indians," that intrepid woman exclaimed, "Had I twenty sons, I should rejoice, were they all so employed, though I should never see them more." [25] Nor did Wesley's father allow

[22] Tyerman, *op. cit.*, p. 431.
[23] John Stoughton, *History of Religion in England* (London: Hodder & Stoughton, 1881), V, 260.
[24] Tyerman, *op. cit.*, pp. 295 ff.
[25] Stoughton, *op. cit.*, VI, 113.

his own zeal for foreign missions to be cooled by the fact that his earlier scheme had not proved practicable. Eleven months before John and Charles Wesley left England on their mission to Georgia, Samuel Wesley wrote to General Oglethorpe, who had recently brought back to England some Indian chiefs and had presented them to George II:

> I had always so dear a love for your colony that if it had been but ten years ago, I would gladly have devoted the remainder of my life and labours to that place, and think I might before this time have conquered the language without which little can be done among the natives, if the Bishop of London would have done me the honour to have sent me thither, as perhaps he then might, but that is now over.[26]

John Wesley's missionary zeal, as Stoughton puts it, "might almost be said to have come to him by inheritance." [27]

Now, what has all this to do with Wesley's Arminianism? Much, I believe. "The world is my parish": these famous words on Wesley's memorial in Westminster Abbey have a peculiarly eighteenth-century ring. They breathe the universalism of the eighteenth century in a far larger sense than the theological, and could scarcely have been uttered in any earlier age. But they also breathe the missionary and evangelical concern which was Wesley's overmastering passion. To execute this concern Wesley needed—could hardly have succeeded apart from—Arminianism. If universalism had not existed, one may almost say, he would have had to invent or discover it. The theology of Calvinism arises, naturally and properly, as a theology of the people of

---
[26] Tyerman, *op. cit.*, p. 428.
[27] *Op. cit.*, VI, 113.

God within the household of God. An Arminian theology arises equally naturally and properly as a theology of mission to the unbeliever.

Among the Puritans of seventeenth-century England not only was any missionary enterprise almost entirely absent but also there was little or no missionary concern. This is apt to surprise us, but our surprise is a measure of the triumph of Arminianism. One of the few Puritans who both put missionary enterprise high among the objects of his prayers and gave ardent support to John Eliot's isolated mission to the American Indians was Richard Baxter. Theologically Baxter was so far from finding rigid Calvinism acceptable that he was frequently charged with being an Arminian. At the end of the eighteenth century, missionary concern at last awoke among English Dissenters. Among those then most prominent in establishing the Baptist Missionary Society and the London Missionary Society were the two men, Andrew Fuller and Edward Williams, who were also leading the way in reducing or modifying the Calvinism still traditional in orthodox Dissent. In neither century is the double interest coincidental. Speaking historically, the missionary overspill of Christianity during the last 170 years would hardly have been possible psychologically but for the Arminianism of the Wesleyan Methodist movement, which first broke down the dikes in the fifty years before that. In turn, one may surmise, Wesley would not have preached Arminianism so fervently but for his missionary passion.

Here lies the answer to our major question concerning the great divide between the two contrasting types of Arminianism in English religion. The Arminianism of the General Baptists and of the Dissenters at large was an Arminianism of the head.

The conclusion that all men will be saved was a logical consequence of argument about the nature of God. There was as yet no thought of missions. Within a theology still largely necessitarian the doctrine that God wills all men to be saved could, in fact, be as inimical to the notion of missions as could the doctrine that God wills only some men to be saved. Such a doctrine of general redemption, moreover, easily came to be associated with a doctrine of general revelation and this, in turn, with the reduction of the importance of the Incarnation in the plan of salvation.

Wesley's Arminianism, on the other hand, and the Arminianism of the Methodist Societies, was an Arminianism of the heart, a precondition of missionary activity undertaken that all men might be saved by the power of Christ. Hence, while the universalism of the Dissenters tended in a direction Unitarian and rationalist, Methodist universalism by its very nature could not do otherwise than remain Christocentric, missionary, and evangelical. The Wesleyan Methodist Missionary Society was founded in 1814, and it is interesting to observe that in 1817, a generation after the founding of the first dissenting missionary society by the Particular Baptists, the General Baptist New Connexion started a mission of their own.[28] The Socinianizing General Baptists made no such move.

By way of conclusion, let us look again at English Quakerism, which is often useful for correcting, or confirming, such general judgements as have suggested themselves to us. The Baptist historian, W. T. Whitley, states that "Friends had originated with George Fox from the General Baptist stratum."[29] This may be

[28] *Encyclopaedia Britannica* (11th ed.; New York: Encyclopaedia Britannica & Company, 1910-11), Missions.
[29] *Op. cit.*, p. xvi.

suspected of being *parti pris*, but it is a fact that many of the first Quakers were what Fox calls "shattered Baptists," and this may in part account for Quaker Arminianism. Whether Baptist in origin or not, the first Quakers were as one in being passionately missionary in their outlook. To the scornful comment that Quaker doctrine was fit to be taken to Turks and heathens, Samuel Fisher retorts that in truth "many Quakers have been" among them, "but few or none of our Chimney-Corner Churchmen that I know of"; [30] and the retort was justified. Two years before publishing his book Fisher and another Quaker had, in fact, set out for Turkey, and, though they came no nearer their destination than Venice, a third Quaker did complete the journey and even had an interview with the Sultan.[31]

At the same time, the Puritan divines who attacked Quakerism were not mistaken in perceiving in the universalism of the Quakers' "light within" a tendency to a reduced Christology, call it "the light of Christ" though Friends might. Samuel Fisher insists that "the Salvation of God is freely given in common to all men, so that every man who will may have it"; and in defense of this position he appeals to what he calls the "strong and serious Asseverations, Complaints, Commands, and seemingly compassionate Compellations" [32] of God in Scripture. This is one thing. His attribution of sufficiency for salvation to what Friends called "that of God in every man" is another thing. In the course of its history Quakerism does in fact reveal within its own society, and in large measure leave unresolved, the same conflict between the two kinds of Arminianism which, in the wider field of English

[30] *Op. cit.*, II, 21.
[31] William C. Braithwaite, *The Beginnings of Quakerism* (2nd. ed.; New York: Cambridge University Press, 1955), pp. 420-28.
[32] Fisher, *op. cit.*, IV, 93-94.

religion generally, has been our subject. In some periods, as in some contemporary groups, a universalism which is Christocentric and evangelical has been continued or revived in Quakerism and has issued in missionary work. In others a more Socinian or humanist universalism is professed, and any genuine missionary concern is then lacking.

I began by suggesting that today we are all Arminians whether we know it or not, and in a sense this is true. It is also true that in England Arminianism, or what Arminianism has turned into, appears to be dead or dying where it lacks missionary concern. Perhaps this is only a particular application of the broader truth that faith without works is dead, and that faith worketh by love.

[4] The Influence of Arminius on American Theology

Gerald O. McCulloh

My first word must be an expression of appreciation to the Remonstrant Brotherhood for the important achievement of calling together the Arminius Symposium. The passing of four centuries since the birth of the great Dutch theologian, Jacobus Arminius, provides a suitable occasion for celebration and ceremonial observance. But in planning a festival of honor which will contribute to a fuller theological understanding of the Christian faith, the Remonstrant Brotherhood is, in this convocation, fulfilling the life purpose of the distinguished Christian in whose name we are convened. We will enter into the lively inquiry concerning the theology of the Protestant Reformation which is stirring the entire realm of Christian theology. Perhaps this convocation will serve to call the attention of Christian scholars to some points of emphasis which might be sadly overlooked in a restudy of the theological positions of Luther and Calvin alone.

This type of festival is not only an occasion of rejoicing in the memory of a great Christian of long ago. It is also a moment when the discussions and disputations which exerted great influence in shaping Protestant Christianity in Holland, England, and America may be heard again to warn against doctrinal neglect or errors and to lead to new understandings of Christian truth. In the theological conversations going on among ecumenically minded Christians there needs to be a clear recognition of the debt we owe to the Christian scholars of the Low Countries and especially to Arminius.

In the theological education and personal development of a person preparing for the ministry of the church, Arminius' emphases upon God's will in Christ to redeem all men, and that portion of responsibility which rests upon the Christian in the life under grace unto sanctification, are essential in the intellectual and spiritual equipment of the man. There is some truth in the observation that to be a good minister to his flock a man must "pray with them as a Calvinist and preach to them like an Arminian." There is vastly more truth in discovering that he must lead his people into the experience of Christ who has died for their justification and Christ living in them for their sanctification. Hence, we rejoice in what this Arminius Symposium may mean in contemporary Christianity.

As a minister of The Methodist Church in the United States, I would add my personal word of appreciation both for the insights and understanding of the way of Christian salvation which have enriched my life and also for that of my denomination which has come to us from Arminius through John Wesley. Under the teaching of my first professor of historical theology, George Croft Cell, whose book *The Rediscovery of John Wesley* was rightly accused of reddening Wesley's cheeks with Calvinist rouge, we were warned against the tendency to work-righteousness and self-salvation which pervaded Methodism when the Reformation doctrine of justification by faith alone was forgotten. Cell did start American Methodists to rereading Calvin. But

Cell's thesis was that the Wesleyan movement was a revolt against the deistic and rationalistic preoccupation of the Anglican Arminianism of Wesley's time. He did not minimize the importance of Wesley's debt to Arminius and Episcopius as well as to Luther and Calvin,[1] or that Wesley called upon Arminius in support of his own doctrinal teaching. Wesley's position, Cell saw clearly, was one of *"evangelical* Arminianism, . . . which he consciously derived from and confidently referred to Arminius himself." [2]

But long before I learned of Arminius in professional theological study, I had been imbued at home with his principles of a universal atonement, a Christocentric view of God's judgments of wrath and mercy, and a prevenient grace in which I might hope. I was taught of a co-operating grace by which I could look for "saving help from a higher source" in the discharge of the responsibility for moral obedience which constrained me as a child of God. I felt a hearty joy in present salvation which we sang of as "blessed assurance," and I knew the expectation of spiritual cleansing and strengthening, which is sanctification, and the perseverance of the saints, which was seen to be in some measure a fruit of their total devotion. I had found in experience that I could be forgiven and be born into new life as a child of God. In this life my freedom was to be exercised in response to a vocation to live in pure and holy love. By the age of ten I had read Wesley's *Plain Account of Christian Perfection*. I was born and reared in a Methodist parsonage where Wesleyan Arminianism was as much a part of my life as was daily bread, family devotions each morning, and grace before meat. Thus, I personally am

---

[1] (New York: Henry Holt & Co., 1935), p. 10.
[2] *Ibid.*, p. 21.

honoring a spiritual forebear in sharing in this Arminius Symposium.

These foregoing remarks are not mere felicitations for the occasion (an amenity of public address which Arminius' writings for various occasions show him never to have neglected). They are intended to serve as concrete examples by way of introduction to the theme assigned to me, namely, "The Influence of Arminius on American Theology."

Among the first settlers in the new world were the Puritans from the village of Scrooby who, after a period of residence in Holland, established the Plymouth Colony in 1620. They had come from a section of England which was deeply dyed with the Puritan reaction against the High-Church Anglicanism of James VI, Charles I, and Archbishop Laud. William Warren Sweet in *The Story of Religion in America* characterizes the section of England from which the early colonists came as,

> The stronghold of Puritanism. . . . The wool-growing district, in close touch with the continent, and especially with the United Netherlands, which had become one of the chief centers of Calvinism. The University of Cambridge was the intellectual center of this region, and many a congregation became completely Puritan under the influence of clergymen educated at Cambridge. . . . The New England leaders were Cambridge men.[3]

Twenty to thirty thousand persons emigrated from this region in the brief period from 1628 to 1642 to settle in New England.

The development of religious ideas and institutions in New England was not, however, a clear and unchallenged establish-

[3] (New York: Harper & Brothers, 1930), pp. 22-23.

ment of high Calvinism even in that section of the colonial settlement. During the first years of life amid the rigors and deprivations of the New World, the sternness of the Puritans' doctrine stood them in firm stead. Frank Hugh Foster in *A Genetic History of New England Theology* makes the following observation:

> The first Puritans, sure in their own hearts that they were the elect of God, found the doctrine [of election] necessary to sustain them in the tremendous struggles through which they passed. . . . Hence the doctrine nerved to greater activity; and it produced a similar effect, during the first period of the promulgation of Calvinism.[4]

In the surety of the absolute sovereignty of God and of their being guided by his hand they survived and kept the faith pure within their own households. They set up a Bible commonwealth with the laws of the Scripture to be administered as the laws of civil relations.

But in the frontier life which was theirs, with the admixture of new immigrants and the touch of trade, they found themselves confronted with a new necessity. These men of faith, who held such high purpose and imposed such high demands upon their households and their ministry, were confronted with a missionary task.[5] The Calvinist correlative of God's absolute sovereignty is man's inability. The faithful discovered that for men who did not hold themselves to be the elect of God, who preferred their frontier roistering to the stiff-necked Puritan morality, the doctrine of man's inability simply confirmed them in their comfort-

---

[4] (Chicago: University of Chicago Press, 1907), p. 29.
[5] *Ibid.*, p. 30.

able acceptance of their waywardness. For some who grew weary under the Puritan demands, the low estimate of their ability was in accord with their evaluation of themselves.

When inability was preached to men who were not conscious that they were the elect, when passive waiting for the gracious deliverance of God was inculcated upon men whom the tide of events no longer forced to activity in spite of themselves and of their theories, it produced sluggishness, apathy, self-distrust, despair. It has never been a good way to induce men to repent to tell them that they cannot.[6]

"The doctrine of inability, so preached as to deplete the churches, by discouraging repentance and faith," caused a serious decline in the close-knit community wholeness of the churches.[7]

By 1648 there was the appearance of doctrinal divergence within the seemingly homogeneous body of New England Calvinism. At the Synod of Cambridge, Puritanism was deliberately rejected in favor of a freer approach to faith and the Scriptures. "The Westminster Confession of Faith was not made binding on the individual churches."[8] The primitive Christian trust in the Scriptures as a guide to faith and order, within the context of the freedom which was in the air of the New World, prevailed. There was a toleration to dissent—to emphasize morality more than purity of doctrine—and a basic, almost individualistic, trust in the guidance of the Scriptures which made it virtually impossible to maintain for long an "ecclesiocracy" of either the Roman Catholic or the European Protestant sort.

A theological challenge to the currently accepted Calvinism and

[6] *Ibid.*, p. 29.
[7] *Ibid.*, p. 43.
[8] Thomas Cuming Hall, *The Religious Background of American Culture* (Boston: Little, Brown & Co., 1930), p. 105.

its theory of the Atonement appeared from an unexpected source. William Pynchon, one of the incorporators of the Massachusetts Colony, published a book in 1650 entitled *The Meritorious Price of Our Redemption*. In it he took issue with the view that Christ in his death bore the wrath of God; he rejected also the theory of imputed guilt and righteousness. Although Pynchon's book was burned, refuted officially by the General Court, its views suppressed, and its author so harassed that he returned to England, yet the seeds had been sown in a colony where thoughtful men were exploring the meaning of their faith.[9] Pynchon made wide use of Scripture to support the view that the justice of God requires only the soul which sins to die. God required and accepted, he says, the mediatorial work of Christ "as satisfactory for the procuring of his atonement for our full redemption, justification, and adoption."[10] Pynchon makes reference to Hugo Grotius and his "governmental" theory of the Atonement. It will be remembered that Grotius was a pupil of Arminius in the days of his teaching at the University of Leiden.

On the American scene there was also a strong sense of individualism which found the Arminian emphases upon freedom and moral responsibility paralleled by the frontier demand upon the individual to move out and take firm hold of life and the land if he would possess it. This quality of Arminianism has been noted by Parrington as one of the reasons for its importance in American Christianity:

Arminianism carried a social significance greater than its theological import: it was an expression of the ideal of individual re-

[9] Foster, *op. cit.*, pp. 16-17.
[10] Pynchon, *The Meritorious Price of Our Redemption*, quoted by Foster, *op. cit.*, p. 17.

sponsibility that emerged from the decay of the feudal system. The first reformers had asserted the right to individual interpretation of the Scriptures; the Arminians threw upon the individual the whole responsibility, bidding him assert his will and achieve his own salvation.[11]

The frontier presented a challenge which faith beyond the bounds of high Calvinism found resources to meet.

In the years and events that followed in the development of New England, freedom of thought, toleration of radical difference of views, and the logical implication of the doctrine of universal rather than limited atonement found expression in the Unitarian and Universalist churches, which remain strong in New England to this day. These churches have recently completed an organic union of their ecclesiastical bodies.

With the turn of the political tide in favor of Puritan dominance in England, it was the Anglicans who left their homelands in great numbers to settle in Virginia, Maryland, and the Carolinas. These colonists, as might be expected, brought with them the Arminian views and influences which had already been accepted by the High-Church party in the Church of England.

Similarly the fortunes of persecution of the Presbyterians in Scotland led to their emigration to Ireland. During the first half of the eighteenth century vast numbers of Scotch-Irish immigrants were finding new homes in the American colonies. With them came predominantly their Presbyterianism in church polity and their Calvinism in doctrine, tempered by their own struggle for freedom of thought and ecclesiastical practice.

[11] Vernon Louis Parrington, *Main Currents in American Thought* (New York: Harcourt, Brace & Co., 1927, 1930), p. 149.

The Dutch colonists came to the new World as a part of the great trading and colonizing boom which followed freedom from Spanish domination and the establishment of the Republic of the United Netherlands. "Having achieved independence, they became at once one of the great commercial and maritime powers of Europe, and Dutch ships were soon finding their way into every port." [12] The colonists from the Low Countries, though few in number, were predominantly Protestant. Although there were among them followers of Luther, Zwingli, and Calvin, the official doctrine and discipline of the Dutch were Calvinistic. Yet the Arminian Remonstrance had been promulgated and its voice was not stilled. Although judgment was rendered against the Remonstrants at the Synod of Dort in 1618-19, within little more than a decade the strictures were relaxed. By 1630 residence and the right of building churches and schools had been accorded to the Remonstrants. The influence of the more liberal views of Arminius was spread abroad with Dutch commerce and colonization.

Probably the clearest and most self-consciously Arminian of all the Christian groups in America, historically, have been the Methodists. Methodist preaching began in an unauthorized way through the Irish immigrants. Whether Methodist meetings were first held in John Street Church in New York by Philip Embury or in a farmer's cottage in rural Maryland by Robert Strawbridge (*ca.* 1766-68)—a dispute of priority that may never be settled—both were Irish Methodists who felt the call of the spirit within themselves and the urging of the situation to preach. And preach they did. By 1769 Wesley sent two preachers from England who

---

[12] Sweet, *op. cit.,* p. 32.

were to carry on the mission in the colonies. It will be remembered that at this time Methodist preaching and the formation of societies were conceived to be within the structure and sacramental order of the Church of England.

After the War of Independence the first religious body to form an independent national church was the Methodists. In 1784 at the Christmas Conference in Baltimore The Methodist Episcopal Church in America was organized. Francis Asbury and Thomas Coke were chosen by Wesley to serve as general superintendents in the organization of Methodism "to spread scriptural holiness throughout the land." Because of both its polity and its doctrine Methodism was remarkably suited for the new country. Methodism developed a ministry that was itinerant, extempore, and hardy enough to keep up with the westward expansion of American settlement. With the Methodist expansion went one of the most significant prongs of Arminian penetration in America. Sweet, a historian rather than a theologian, gives an overdrawn but vivid impression of Methodist Arminianism moving westward:

The doctrine preached by the Methodist circuit riders was also well adapted to meet the hearty acceptance of the frontiersman. It was a gospel of free will and free grace, as opposed to the doctrines of limited grace, and predestination preached by the Calvinistic Presbyterians, or even the milder Calvinism of the Baptists. The frontier Methodist preachers brought home to the pioneers the fact that they were masters of their own destiny, an emphasis which fitted in exactly with the new democracy rising in the West, for both emphasized the actual equality of all men.[13]

[13] *Ibid.*, p. 317.

This westward march of Methodist preaching had moved as far as Tennessee in mid-continent with the formation of the Holsten Circuit in 1783, a year before the historic Christmas Conference of 1784 when American Methodism was officially born.

The Arminianism of the Methodist preachers was not accidental, nor merely an expedient adjustment to the exigencies of frontier life. Wesley sent to America twenty-four Articles of Religion to guide the newly-formed church, an edited form of the thirty-nine Articles of the Church of England from which many of the Calvinistic emphases had been carefully excised. He bequeathed to American Methodism a general Arminian theology which placed emphasis upon free will, universal atonement, gracious ability, the witness of the spirit, and the possibility of falling from grace.[14] By 1789 the Conference, just five years old, was publishing and sponsoring the reading of Baxter's *A Call to the Unconverted* and *The Saints' Everlasting Rest*, Fletcher's *Checks to Antinomanism*, and John Wesley's hymn books, sermons, and *Notes on the New Testament*. The first periodical begun was *The Arminian Magazine*, a short-lived venture which was followed by *The Methodist Magazine*, and *The Methodist Quarterly Review*.

In the early part of the nineteenth century, Nathan Bangs (1778-1845), book editor for the Methodists in America, published a *Life of Arminius* based on the Nichols edition of the *Oration of Bertius* and excerpts from Brandt's *The Life of James Arminius, D.D.* He kept a constant flow of Arminian theology running through the pages of *The Methodist Quarterly Review* and into the ministers' *Course of Study* of which he was the founder. He

[14] John Fletcher Hurst, *History of Methodism* (New York: Eaton and Mains, 1902-04), V, 822.

was a prolific writer, a champion of Arminianism, and a highly influential force in Methodism for half a century.[15]

The Methodist theological writers of the nineteenth century, to whom the earlier reading of Richard Watson's *Theological Institutes* and Wesley's sermons and notes on the Old and New Testaments gave place, were Wilbur F. Tillett, Miner Raymond, Thomas O. Summers, Daniel D. Whedon, John Miley, William Fairfield Warren, Randolph S. Foster, Olin A. Curtis, and Borden Parker Bowne. In all of these the influence of Arminianism is traceable, and for many Arminius was acknowledged to be the theological forebear of the Wesleyanism which they championed. Thomas O. Summers in 1857 published an American edition of Brandt's *The Life of James Arminius, D.D.* and wrote an introduction for it. His own two volume systematic theology shows by its title, *Systematic Theology: A Complete Body of Wesleyan Arminian Divinity,* the theology he intended to propound. "Summers distinguishes, as did Augustine, preventing and co-operating grace. Preventing grace gives man 'the capacity to will and to do the right, enlightening the intellect,' and co-operating grace 'works in us, of course, but it cannot work in us, *after the initial operation,* without working with us.' "[16] Man's responsibility was stressed in Arminian language.

In the twentieth century the emphasis on free will and man's responsibility continues in American Methodism in such theological teachers as Albert C. Knudson, Harris F. Rall, the earlier writings

---

[15] Abel Stevens, *Life and Times of Nathan Bangs, D.D.* (New York: Carlton & Porter, 1863), pp. 13-15.

[16] David Clark Shipley, "Development of Theology in American Methodism in the Nineteenth Century," *The London Quarterly and Holborn Review* (July, 1959), p. 259.

of Edwin Lewis, and the recent *Case for Theology in Liberal Perspective* of L. Harold DeWolf.

The influence of Arminianism was felt in the West within Presbyterianism also. The minister of the First Presbyterian Church in Nashville, Tennessee, was dismissed within five years of the founding of the church for Arminian views departing from Calvinism. The Cumberland Presbyterian Church separated from the parent church and remains a force in the southern United States. Its reasons for separation were to meet the frontier needs by the use of itinerant clergy who could not meet the formal educational requirements and to soften the rigors of Calvinist election with a doctrine of free and universal grace. The Arminian source of these views did not go unrecognized.

Other denominational traditions which show clear historical evidence of Arminian influence are the Free Will Baptists, the American Mennonites, the Unitarians, the Univeralists, and several of the Holiness and Pentecostal groups. Probably the most evangelical of these is the Church of the Nazarene, which has carried a continuing Arminian interest. This interest is seen in the theological writings of Henry O. Wiley, Timothy L. Smith, and Carl O. Bangs. Dr. Bangs has performed the most recent scholarly service in American Arminian studies in his unpublished thesis, "Arminius and the Reformation Theology," which was presented at the University of Chicago in 1958. His bibliography of Arminian materials is probably the most complete that has ever been compiled.

An interesting example of the way the influence of Arminius has moved in America is to be seen in the development of the groups which have stressed the doctrine of sanctification. It should not be understood that the holiness groups stressed sanctification because it was Arminian. The interest of these groups inclined rather to the doctrine because it was a rallying point of subjectivism and individual experience in contrast to what they called formality, worldiness, and coldness within the churches. In mid-nineteenth century the camp-meeting fever was unabated, and personal spiritual holiness was one of the experiences most earnestly sought. The influence of Arminius' doctrine of sanctification upon the American revival movement is clear and vital. This was true in various denominational communions, as seen for example in Congregationalism through Nathaniel W. Taylor at Yale and Charles G. Finney at Oberlin College, and the holiness emphasis in Methodism.

When the holiness party, which had found a place in most of the evangelical denominations, was not able to prevail in determining the spirit and practice of the entire denomination, then those most eager proponents of holiness began to form holiness associations, hold holiness meetings, engage holiness preachers and evangelists, and establish and hold their own camp meetings. In the last decade of the nineteenth century no fewer than "ten separate religious bodies were organized with entire sanctification as their cardinal doctrine." [17] Such groups appeared from New York City to Los Angeles, both North and South. The Church of the Nazarene gathered more than half of these new church groups into a single organization in 1907-8. It is scarcely accidental that theological teachers of the Church of the Nazarene have begun serious exploration of the roots of their doctrine and are giving renewed study to the works of Arminius.

Arminius wrote of sanctification as follows:

[17] John Leland Peters, *Christian Perfection and American Methodism* (Nashville: Abingdon Press, 1956), p. 148.

[Sanctification] is a gracious act of God, by which he purifies man who is a sinner, and yet a believer, from the darkness of ignorance, from indwelling sin and its lusts or desires, and imbues him with the Spirit of knowledge, righteousness, and holiness, that, being separated from the life of the world and made conformable to God, man may live the life of God, to the praise of the righteousness and of the glorious grace of God, and to his own salvation.[18]

For a holiness partisan to come upon such a passage is to find a wellspring of his "water of life." The champions of sanctification were numerous and vocal at the opening of the twentieth century in America. They were in an important respect, though perhaps unconsciously, one of the manifestations of the influence of Arminius.

If there were not another paper in this symposium on the influence of Arminius on social issues, I should be tempted to trace the effect of Arminius' thought upon the social gospel movement in the early twentieth century. It is sufficient perhaps to note that the Christian man's acceptance of the responsibility for social evil and his search for a social redemption through a process of individual and social Christian nurture suggest the shaping hand of Arminius' doctrine of man's responsible participation in growth and development in the life of grace. And certainly Grotius, Arminius' pupil, exerted a strong influence on the emerging concept of salvation as a social experience.

During the second quarter of the twentieth century American theology took a different turn. The theological revival turned the Christian scholars' interest again to Luther and Calvin. Under the influence of neo-orthodoxy optimistic humanism began to surrender to a widely proclaimed view of man as sin. Though

[18] *Writings*, II, 120.

man is not necessarily a sinner, yet inevitably he is a sinner because he is a victim of the human predicament. Man can escape his plight only through justification by faith. Faith is not a response in which man takes an active and determinative part. It is a state into which he is transformed by a gracious act of God. Revelation is not through reason, but often is in direct contradiction to it. For man to attempt to use reason to search for God, or to attempt to will moral obedience and thus please God, is self-idolatry. Man came to be viewed as a creature in absolute disjunction from his Creator. The doctrinal views of Calvin are often quoted and proclaimed. But Arminius' pleas for reason and tolerance; his insistence upon the dignity and freedom of man as born under a prevenient grace, because even as in Adam all died, so in Christ have all been made alive; his view of man's responsibility to persevere in faith and obedience, albeit able to fall through his own fault and perish upon his own failure rather than Adam's guilt; his recognition of the rightful place of the assurance of present salvation; and his vocation to grow in individual and social righteousness in the experience of sanctification—all these are stilled. The voice of the inspiration to remonstrance against an absolute and unconditional divine sovereignty, limited atonement, the irresistibility of grace—this voice is not heard in the land. Arminius' name is almost completely absent from the tables of contents or the indexes of the most recent widely read works in theology. In American theology the time is ripe for a new remonstrance.

In this final section I wish to note some characteristics of the American mind and indicate those elements in the doctrinal position of Arminius which are related to these characteristic American ideas. The tracing of direct lines of influence will not be attempted, because it would be lengthy and tiresome. In many cases it would be speculative and roundabout. Nevertheless, I believe the influence of the Arminian understanding of Christian doctrine and life to have been at work in many ways. And undoubtedly some of the ideas cited have developed far beyond the intention or desire of Arminius himself. Arthur Cushman McGiffert said of the Arminian movement that: "There was more in the movement than appeared on the surface. . . . There was in the movement the promise of a greater break [with Calvinism] to come, the prophecy of an application of the modern principle in a way to overthrow the old completely." [19] That the modern principles can or should overthrow Calvinism completely must be questioned. That the developments stemming from Arminianism have broken away from Calvinism in many important respects more completely than Arminius himself broke with Calvin is beyond question. We turn to a summary of some of the views to be found in American Christianity, which took their inspiration from Arminius but which in development have been carried much further perhaps than Arminius would be willing to go. Their direction and dynamics, however, were found in the doctrines of the Dutch reformer.

The first of these patterns in the American mind concerns belief about God and his nature. There is widespread acceptance that God is the determiner of the order of reality, that he is involved in the world's struggle and concerned with the problems of all people. The order of nature is an arena in which he is active and may be known through the exercise of reason. In

[19] *Protestant Thought Before Kant* (New York: Charles Scribner's Sons, 1951), p. 189.

accordance with God's will and his grace, man may respond in faith and live in an awareness of and communion with him. God is just and righteous and demands obedience in thought and action that relate to moral goodness. The struggle with nature and with evil of the early colonists and of our twentieth-century contemporaries alike finds them convinced that, in their continuing encounter, God is their ally. God, in the sending of his Son into the world, entered this earthly enterprise for its salvation and continues his providence and his redemptive and sanctifying concern for the children of men.

Arminius' doctrine of God portrays him as providentially preserving, regulating, governing, and directing all things; nothing in the world happens apart from him.[20] To Arminius God is the most excellent object of knowledge, lucid and clear to the mind, unfolding himself to reason and the mental powers.[21] He manifests himself to the external senses, the inward fancy or imagination, and to the mind or understanding.[22] The attributes of God's nature have their analogies in man's moral virtues, such as justice, righteousness, truth, sincerity, fidelity, patience, long-suffering, gentleness, and leniency or readiness to forgive.[23] Man's response is to be made in knowledge, faith, trust, and obedience. The subject of faith is the mind, that is, theoretical understanding and also the practical affections.[24] It is self-evident that the relation of these Arminian ideas to the above-mentioned characteristic modes of American Christian thought are as the root system is to the tree that grows upon it.

[20] *Writings*, I, 251.
[21] *Ibid.*, pp. 57-60.
[22] *Ibid.*, p. 98.
[23] *Ibid.*, II, 48-49.
[24] *Ibid.*, pp. 109 ff.

As a second characteristic of American Christian thought we can cite the belief in a universal atonement, intended for all through the mediatorship of Christ in his incarnation, his life and teachings, his death and resurrection. One would need to search far beyond any of the major groups of American Christians today to find adherents of a doctrine of double predestination or of election that is not contingent upon man's response in faith to God's universal will to redeem all.

In Arminius' view of universal atonement and his rejection of a doctrine of predestination which stems from a decree of God apart from any consideration of man's response to the proffered atonement, he departed perhaps most clearly and outspokenly from Calvin, Bèze and Junius.[25] Here also American Christianity exhibits Arminian rather than Calvinist leanings.

Thirdly, to the American mind conversion to the Christian faith is counterfeit unless it is followed by a long and faithful reordering of the life of the believer in fulfillment of his profession. The power for this purification of life is not man's own. He must rely upon and obey the Holy Spirit present and working within him. There is by no means universal agreement among American Christians that man's life, even by the assistance of the Holy Spirit, may be expected to achieve perfection or—as it is variously called—entire sanctification. Such an expectation was long a characteristic of Methodist preaching with its Arminian roots. This doctrine is seldom expounded in present-day American Methodism. But the expectation which Arminius seems to have meant by sanctification, that is, spiritual and moral growth in faith and obedience after justification, is a part of the typical

[25] *Ibid*, I, 316.

American expectation of practical results. In some circles this sanctification which displays the effective aftermath of conversion would be cited as a phase of Christian pragmatism.

The roots of this view are in Arminius' doctrine of sanctification wherein, by the continuing gracious and empowering presence of the Spirit of God, any man who is a believer is cleansed from sin and comes to "live the life of God, to the praise of righteousness, and of the glorious grace of God."[26] Sanctification is not completed in a single moment. Sin is progressively weakened, and the inner man is day by day renewed more and more.[27]

A fourth characteristic of American Christianity, shared with the political ideology of the nation and the predisposition of the American people, is the belief in the freedom and responsibility of man under divine grace. It would be a mistake to cite this belief of American Christians as an example of the corruption of the religious mind through the acceptance of a secular ideal. The principle of liberty in American thought was expressed in terms of its divine source as early as the Declaration of Independence by the American colonies. Thomas Jefferson and his fellow revolutionaries wrote in the Declaration of Independence: "We hold these truths to be self-evident, that all men are created equal, that they are endowed by their Creator with certain unalienable Rights, that among these are Life, Liberty and the Pursuit of Happiness." The four freedoms of recent popular acclaim—freedom from want, freedom from fear, freedom of speech, and free-

---

[26] *Ibid.,* II, 120.
[27] Carl O. Bangs, "Arminius and the Reformation Theology" (Unpublished thesis, University of Chicago, 1958), p. 177.

dom of religion—demonstrate how fondly the founding principle of freedom is still held in the American scene. Although Henry David Thoreau's essay on "Civil Disobedience" is widely read and studied, the carrying of freedom to the level of a claim of immunity from law in civil life or antinomianism in religious life is not generally acceptable. The freedom which the American holds dear is freedom under God's grace and his nation's laws.

Arminius held that God proffers his gift of grace like a rich man giving alms, and also that man must responsibly and freely accept this grace like the poor man reaching to receive them. If God gave his grace, he contended, in such a way as to make it irresistible he would add to grace that which is not grace.[28] God will not violate the freedom he gives to man even to prevent sin. The overriding of man's freedom to prevent sin "would be absolutely contrary to the good of the universe, inasmuch as one good of the universe consists even in this, that there should be a creature endued with free will, and that the use of his own free will should be conceded to the creature without any divine interference."[29] "By no Divine decree is the human will determined either to the one side or the other."[30] "There are two stumblingblocks," said Arminius, "against which I am solicitously on my guard,—not to make God the author of sin, and not to do away with the freedom inherent in the human will."[31] This respect of God for the freedom he has granted to man includes the permission of disobedience and falling from grace, even totally and

[28] *Writings*, I, 365-66.
[29] *Ibid.*, III, 302.
[30] Arminius, *Letter* to Junius, quoted by Casper Brandt, *Life of James Arminius, D.D.*, trans. John Guthrie (Nashville: Publishing House of the Methodist Episcopal Church, South, 1908), p. 157.
[31] *Ibid.*, p. 222.

finally.³² Cognate to the idea of freedom is the spirit of religious toleration. This is expressed in American parlance as "freedom of religion." It finds its parallel likewise in Arminius' championing of toleration of dissent, both in principle and in practice.³³

The fifth and last emphasis in American Christian thought to be cited in this summary is that man is responsible for living in the world in such a way that he shares in the community of the kingdom of God. In its more energetic form this conviction gave rise to the Social Gospel Movement. In its more unguarded expressions, it was given to the assumption that man by his own devotion and righteous acts could "establish" or "build" the kingdom of God on earth. There have also been American attempts to establish communities under theocratic or ecclesiocratic rule but these have not been eminently successful nor widely accepted. Between these two extremes there is a strong conviction in American Christianity that, acting within the context of separation of church and state, Christians have a responsibility to inculcate Christian principles in their daily associations. In Christian obedience, both individual holiness and social righteousness are the vocation of the man of faith.

Concerning salvation in Christ, Arminius wrote: "It requires to be received, understood, believed, fulfilled in deed and reality." ³⁴ "What employment is more becoming and honorable in a creature, a servant, and a son, than to spend his whole days and nights in obtaining a knowledge of God his Creator, his Lord, and his Father?" ³⁵ Obedience has three parts; to the first,

---
³² *Writings*, I, 385; II, 46, 502.
³³ Bangs, *op. cit.*, p. 36; Hall, *op. cit.*, p. 105.
³⁴ *Writings*, I, 109.
³⁵ *Ibid.*, p. 79.

MAN'S FAITH AND FREEDOM

which is repentance, and the second, which is faith, must be joined the third, which is the "observance of God's commands." Thus obedience culminates in "holiness of life, to which believers are called, and without which no man shall see God." [36] Obedience, Arminius further says, is the formal object of all the divine precepts.[37] When the intellect, affections, and will have been renewed, then man is qualified and required to understand, esteem, consider, will, and perform whatever is truly good.[38] Then shall follow one of the results of the kingly work of Christ in the gathering of the church, the calling of the Gentiles, and the restoration of the Jews. In such redemptive tasks within the world, faith answers to its divine vocation.[39]

The language of contemporary American Christianity is different, but the vocation to live in obedience, extend the church, and practice righteousness in society has its parallel in the teaching of the great Dutch theologian.

The recent revival of theological interest in America, as has been previously noted, is centering upon the study and promulgation of the theology of the Reformers, notably Luther and Calvin. But the doctrines of unconditional predestination, irresistible grace, and a limited atonement are notably omitted from the revival. Arminius apparently has made his case in exposing error and in propounding truth in Christian understanding. It re-

[36] *Ibid.*, II, 107.
[37] *Ibid.*, p. 169.
[38] *Ibid.*, I, 252.
[39] *Ibid.*, II, 91.

mains for his name and his work to be accorded its deserved recognition and revival in the ecumenical conversation in contemporary Christendom. The fulfillment of this need may, it is hoped, be one of the long-range results of this Arminius Symposium.

[5] Arminius and the Structure of Society

James Luther Adams

Not as a total stranger does the citizen of Massachusetts visit Amsterdam, a seat of the old Dutch Republic. Not as a stranger does a member of Harvard University join in this celebration of the four-hundredth anniversary of Jacobus Arminius. Many are the spiritual children of the Dutch Republic and also of Arminius who have contributed to the heritage of Massachusetts and of America in both politics and religion. Permit me as a representative of American Unitarianism to express my hearty appreciation for the privilege of participating in this anniversary celebration and for the warm and generous hospitality I and my colleagues have enjoyed here at the hands of the Remonstrant Brotherhood.

It is now just over a century since the Boston scholar John Lothrop Motley first published *The Rise of the Dutch Republic* (1856). A few years later he published *The History of the United Netherlands,* and then about a decade later came his *Life and Death of John of Barneveld.* In honor of Motley, the Queen of the Netherlands set a house apart for his use at The Hague, where he had long labored in the archives. Motley told a Dutch scholar that in preparing these volumes he was struck with the analogies between the emergence of the United Provinces and of the United States and between William of Orange and George Washington. "If ten people in the world," he said, "hate despotism a little more and love civil and religious liberty a little better in consequence of what I have written, I shall be satisfied." By reason of the warm reception accorded his books, Motley was entitled to feel well satisfied, even though Calvinists (like Prinsterer in the Netherlands) severely criticized him for his sympathy with the Arminian cause.

Long before this time, however, the epic of the Dutch Republic and of the conflicts between the Remonstrants and the Contra-Remonstrants was a familiar story in America. Indeed, these things were well known in the American colonies from the beginning, for many of the first colonists migrated to New England only after a sojourn in Holland. Two members of the first Harvard Board of Overseers had been pastors of English churches in the Low Countries; and the first head of Harvard College, Nathaniel Eaton, was an alumnus of the University of Franeker. From Harvard's beginning in 1636 the Dutch universities and scholars were highly esteemed.

The attitude toward Arminianism which prevailed in New England in the seventeenth century, and even later, was expressed in a prayer on behalf of Harvard College which pleaded that the college might be "so tenacious of the truth that it shall be easier to find a wolf in England or a snake in Ireland than a Socinian or Arminian in Cambridge." So far as Cambridge and Harvard were concerned, however, the petition was denied in the end. In the year 1805 the Unitarian Henry Ware was appointed Hollis Professor of Divinity at Harvard, one event, among others, that signalized the successful penetration into the American colonies of ideas that were labeled Arminian. The Harvard Divinity

School as a special division of the university was established in 1816, and from the beginning the *Ars Critica* of the Arminian Jean Le Clerc was staple reading.[1] Already more than half a century before this, Charles Chauncy, the minister of the First Church in Boston and the great-grandson and namesake of the second president of Harvard College, had been a major opponent of the Calvinist Jonathan Edwards and was thus a key figure in the advancement of Arminianism.

By this time, however, the term *Arminian* had become a loose label, a *Kampfbegriff*, not always having a strict connection with the Trinitarian theology of Arminius himself and sometimes implying a Pelagianism that Arminius would have repudiated. Aside from these considerations, we should observe that Arminianism was a composite movement, composite in its historical antecedents and many faceted in its thrust in each of the countries in which it played a role. Indeed, the very openness of discussion which was initially promoted by Arminius and which has characterized the later developments gave to Arminianism its creative and dynamic tensions. Accordingly, the term "Arminian," even when carefully defined, has assumed many shades of meaning.

Consider the variety of ingredients to be found in the antecedents of Arminianism and in the early development. From the outset Arminianism transcended the boundaries of Calvinism as delineated in Geneva. Not only the Dutch Lutherans (and Melanchthon also) were a part of the formative background; Arminianism also presupposed the experience of the sectarians,

---

[1] Le Clerc, born in Geneva, was a teacher at the Seminary in Amsterdam. He was a friend of John Locke and of other leading Whigs in England and was also very sympathetic to the developing interest in the natural sciences. His *Ars Critica* is a study of the new historical criticism of ancient texts. Cf. Colie, *op. cit.*

the practical discipleship, and the struggle for toleration among the Anabaptists and the Mennonites. It presupposed also the spirit of Erasmus, "the philosophy of Christ," an ethical teaching that claimed to be available to reasonable men everywhere, a teaching to be appropriated through free inquiry and through the cultivation of the mind. In the famous school of the *Devotio Moderna* in Utrecht Arminius acquired his classical learning, and from it he gained also his conception of a divinely derived "good conscience" and Christian liberty. Erasmus previously had also attended this school of the Brethren of the Common Life. Moreover, already within its first generation, Arminianism became the name of a High-Church, anti-Puritan movement in the Church of England. At the same time it figured in the development of the left-wing movements of seventeenth-century England.

Subsequently, Arminianism in the various countries was to promote ideas we associate with the Enlightenment; and, later, it was to be adopted with one accent or another by Methodists, and still later by Congregationalists and Unitarians. From its outset, then, Arminianism had roots in the Renaissance and in the left wing as well as in the right wing of the Reformation.

It has been the genius of Arminianism to maintain the discussion between these perspectives and those of the Enlightenment and of the Evangelical Awakening and eventually between these perspectives and those of modern higher criticism and of the modern scientific outlook. Accordingly, the essence of Arminianism is not easy to define, for it has entered into a variety of alliances. In general, it has promoted "a free and catholic spirit" that has cherished practical morality as a sign of the Christian way. This spirit is not to be grasped merely by listing doctrines that are the opposite of those set forth in the Articles of the Synod of

Dort. We can say that it was initially informed by some such gestalt of ideas as the following: the Christian must place his confidence in the sovereignty and the mercy of God; all that is worthy in human life depends upon his grace; salvation through Christ is available to all men; faith precedes election; yet the regenerate man derives from Christ the grace to respond to the offer of salvation; and from Christ he derives also Christian liberty. These doctrines, to be sure, come short of indicating adequately the complex of ideas and practices which has appeared under the rubric of Arminianism.

Previous lectures in the symposium have delineated certain of the basic theological and ethical ideas of Arminianism. We are now to consider broadly some of the social issues that have been the rallying points of the movement. Ideally, one should attempt systematically to relate the theological doctrines to these social issues. Because of limitations of time we must in the main confine attention here to conceptions and practices that bear especially upon the internal organization of the church and also that reveal characteristic tendencies with respect to social organization in general. In the course of the narrative we shall see ample cause for the view of Motley that the whole epic bespeaks a persistent hatred of despotism and a love for civil and religious liberty. More specifically, we shall see that Arminianism has been a major force in the development of those principles of individuation (or differentiation) which belong to modern culture and a major force also in the development of that characteristic preference of a radically Protestant ethos—the preference for what is called freedom of association. Indeed, we shall see that in the history of Arminianism individual freedom and freedom of association are inseparable in principle, for they are mutually interdependent.

ARMINIUS AND THE STRUCTURE OF SOCIETY

In the remarkable Arminius Exhibition arranged at Oudewater, Holland, for the celebration of the present anniversary, one encounters a striking cartoon of the Synod of Dort at which the Remonstrants were condemned. In this cartoon one sees Calvin's *Institutes* and the role of the Advocate John of Barneveld in the scales at the synod as if they were being weighed against each other. The *Institutes* outweighs the robe, the momentary symbol of the Remonstrants, but alongside the *Institutes* in the scale is the sword of Prince Maurice of Orange who took the side of the Contra-Remonstrants. The *sword* tips the balance. The symbols or these scales, the robe and the sword, bespeak the mixture of politics and religion in the whole controversy.

In Holland the sword of brute force had already figured largely in theological controversy for several generations preceding the Synod of Dort. Anyone who has read the Remonstrant Gerard Brandt's seventeenth-century *History of the Reformation in the Low-Countries* (1677) will have an indelible image of the torture to which the Anabaptists, the Calvinists, and other precursors of the Arminians were subjected in the preceding century. Here one encounters a striking illustration of the "natural history" of the Reformation period. So much was coercion in the ascendant that in most countries it determined the immediate victory. The Swiss historian Jakob Burckhardt has reminded us that the religious confession that prevailed in each territory of Europe was the one that commanded the strongest battalions. So also, following the Synod of Dort, the Calvinists harried the Remonstrants out of the land. Although these Calvinists had themselves previously pleaded for religious liberty in face of Roman Catholic Spanish tyranny, and although they themselves had suffered persecution, they retained the policies of the church fanatical when their turn came to control the power. In face of this heritage of coercion, Arminius and his associates a generation before the meeting of the Synod of Dort had tried, as was said of Erasmus, "to reform the Reformers and the Reformation itself."[2] They started a third Reformation.

We should not forget, however, that in attempting this reformation Arminius remained in certain fundamental respects a Calvinist. He retained the conviction of the sovereignty of God, the sense of man's ultimate dependence upon God in Christ, the protest against the idolatry that gives to the creature the devotion that belongs to God alone, the strong moral passion, and the demand for social order.

At the same time he was vividly sensitive to the power of God which manifests itself in compassion and tenderness, to the power that gives a new liberty in the gospel. Arminius took seriously the promise, "And I, if I be lifted up from the earth, will draw all men unto me." We may say that affection, attraction, or love, rather than will was the fundamental *pathos* of his life-view. Through God's providence and love man has freedom to accept or reject the power unto salvation in Jesus Christ. Sören Kierkegaard would very much have liked this element of the freedom of love in the thought and life of Arminius. Kierkegaard asserts that the omnipotence of God is to be seen not in his absolute control of creation but rather in his power to bring into being a

[2] Gerard Brandt, *The History of the Reformation and Other Ecclesiastical Transactions in and About the Low-Countries*. Trans. from the Low-Dutch (London: T. Wood, 1720), I, 73. Brandt in this work reflects the Dutch Arminianism of the latter part of the seventeenth century. Constantly appealing to Erasmus, he favors tolerance in place of coercion, mutual forbearance notwithstanding "diversity in points not fundamental," and simplicity of doctrine, sanctioned (he believes) by the practice of the early church, "the primitive model."

creature that can turn against him and that can voluntarily turn towards him.

Arminius, appealing to Lactantius, held that: "To recommend faith to others, we must make it the subject of persuasion, and not of compulsion." He insisted that the true religion from Christ does not deteriorate into dissension. In the exercise of Christian liberty there will be sincere and honest differences. These differences cannot and should not be stamped out by means of coercion. In confronting the Scripture, Christians should be able to agree on what is necessary for salvation. But when mutual consent and agreement cannot be obtained on some articles, "then the right hand of fellowship should be extended by both parties." Each party should "acknowledge the other for partakers of the same faith and fellow-heirs of the same salvation, although they may hold different sentiments concerning the nature of faith and the manner of salvation." [3] It is the obligation of the magistrates to maintain the conditions for this sort of discussion in synod. Arminius favored not only freedom of discussion and sweet reasonableness on the basis of the broad fundamentals of Christian faith; he wished also that the synod would eschew idolatry in its attitude toward itself and its decisions. He held that even if the synod were to achieve unanimous decision, it should not impose it upon others by force, for it is possible that even with unanimous decision the synod might have "committed an error in judgment." Such an error can appear in the realm of discipline as well as of doctrine. Accordingly, a synod, he believed, should leave open the way for revision of its findings. How characteristic it is for Arminius to conclude his ecclesiological *Disputation LVI* (Corollary) with this question:

[3] *Writings*, I, 188, 189.

Is it not useful, for the purpose of bearing testimony to the power and the liberty of the church, occasionally to make some change in the laws ecclesiastical, lest the observance of them becoming perpetual, and without any change, should produce an opinion of the (absolute) necessity of their being observed? [4]

Arminius wanted a church free from bondage to itself.

For Arminius the love of truth should under God liberate men from this bondage. As against those who would make the Dutch Confession mandatory, the Arminians appealed to Scripture as the broader, sounder norm of faith. As members of the Reformed movement, they were set against the idolatry of both the Roman Catholics and the high Calvinists who permitted their teachers and their confessions to separate them from direct examination of Scripture. In this they could appeal for sanction to Calvin himself. Without freedom of faith, Arminius asserts, the Reformation itself could not have come into being, and without it the Reformation could become inured to error. Therefore, he held that the presidency of the free assembly should be the Holy Spirit, "for he has promised to be present where even two or three are gathered in His name." This is "the true, free assembly most appropriate for the investigation of truth and the establishment of concord." Over the porch of the assembly, he says, this sentence, after the manner of Plato, should be inscribed in letters of gold: "Let no one enter this hallowed dome without a desire for the truth and for peace." Otherwise, he says, religion will experience "almost the same fate as the young lady mentioned by Plutarch,

[4] *Ibid.*, II, 140. I am indebted to Carl Bangs of the Olivet Nazarene College, Kankakee, Illinois, for calling this Disputation to my attention and for other instruction regarding the outlook of Arminius. His dissertation on Arminius, prepared at the University of Chicago, is to be published presently. Dr. Bangs attended the symposium and participated in the panel discussions.

who was addressed by a number of suitors; and when each of them found that she could not become entirely his own, they divided her body into parts, and thus not one of them obtained possession of her whole person."[5] Here we detect the spirit of Erasmus who strove for the Christian and human virtues of tolerance and peace and love of neighbor.

Arminius was resolved to resist the contentious spirit common in the theological debates of his time. "Invective, mutual anathematizing and execration," he felt, would not "excite the minds of people to the love and study of truth, to charity, mercy, longsuffering and concord." He took a dim view of the method of disputation which was then prevalent in the universities. He wished that the discussion of matters of faith could be conducted in such a fashion that the observer might exclaim, "See how these Christians love one another." A favorite word of Arminius was "moderation."

In demanding that toleration be protected by the magistrates Arminius was scarcely advocating a novelty, even among the Calvinists. Charles Perrot, a liberal theologian in Geneva, had advised Uitenbogaert, a friend of Arminius: "Never assist in condemning any for not agreeing in every point of religion with the established church, so long as they adhere to the fundamentals of Christianity, and are disposed to maintain the peace." To be sure, the issue that is difficult to determine is the question as to what the fundamentals are.

Among the Dutch "Churches under the Cross" the writings of Erasmus with their plea for toleration had been popular for two generations. These churches had included the magistrates and laymen in the direction of church affairs. Jasper Coolhaes,

[5] *Ibid.*, pp. 161-62 .

formerly a member of the faculty at Leiden, had been protected by the magistrates when he advocated tolerance for Lutherans and Anabaptists and even for disciples of Bèze. Arminius himself probably would not have received his appointment to the Leiden faculty if the magistrates had not been in control. Men of this tradition relied upon the magistrates, the laity, to protect diversity, for they feared the rigid conformity that would ensue if a clerically controlled consistory of the Bèze preference were in power.

Now, if we are to understand the social issues at stake here, we must view these developments within their broad historical context and implication. What we have been reviewing is part of the process of differentiation or individuation which in varying ways was emerging all over Europe, a process decisively initiated by the Renaissance and by the Reformation in its various branches. This process of differentiation distinguishes an open society from a merely traditionalist society; it is indispensable for the appearance of a free society. At the time of Arminius, however, it was a relatively new movement. Indeed, it represented a revolutionary change. The kind of toleration defended by Arminius and his forebears was moving away from the traditional conception of the Christian commonwealth, the conception of *corpus Christianum*.

According to this traditional conception (introduced by the Emperor Theodosius about the year 378), the stability of society requires uniformity of religious belief. In the Middle Ages the pope and the emperor had been theoretically partners in the task of maintaining society and church in unity. To this end the emperor had been expected to wield the sword against heretics and schismatics. Here the political and the ecclesiastical forces were in alliance, giving rise to a territorial religion. Indeed, Augustine would have called it a civic religion. This conception of territorial religion was not abandoned by the major branches of the Reformation. It was transferred as it were from the whole of Christendom to the parts. Accordingly, Dissenters were banished or persecuted. This territorialism involved state establishment, or recognition of an officially sanctioned group.

The situation was essentially the same in the American colonies, except in Rhode Island and Pennsylvania. Each colony officially recognized only one confession: in Massachusetts and Connecticut the Congregationalists, in New York and New Jersey the Presbyterians, in Maryland the Roman Catholics. The Constitution of the United States which was instituted in 1787 did not change the pattern of establishment in the states, although no religion was to be established in the nation as a whole.

The system of territorialism was mitigated by a marked degree of freedom and variety during the rise of the Dutch Republic. But territorialism was brought back with a vengeance immediately after the Synod of Dort. In this period dissenters, including the Arminians, were subjected to persecution or to legal penalties. The location in Amsterdam of the first Remonstrant edifice of 1630 behind the houses of the Keizersgracht illustrates one of these penalties (familiar also in England in the succeeding period).

Arminius died over twenty years before the construction of this edifice in Amsterdam. Indeed, he died almost a decade before the Synod of Dort. In his view of the church he had not broken completely with the tradition of territorialism. He favored what is now called comprehension. This pattern permits a degree of latitude within the recognized confession; in addition, it permits some leeway to nonconforming groups, though it imposes one penalty or another upon them. The degree of freedom made possible by comprehension is well illustrated in the adoption of Arminian ideas in the Church of England during the early part of the seventeenth century, during the time of the Cambridge Platonists later in this century, and during the period of the Latitudinarians in the eighteenth century.[6]

Although this system of comprehension does not constitute complete religious liberty for all, it does represent an advance in freedom within the internal structure of the established church. The system as it operated in Holland in the seventeenth century was very complex, and we cannot deal with it in detail here. We should note, however, that by reason of the role of the magistrates, political authority was given a place that to us is questionable. We cannot accept this Erastian position. On the other hand, Arminius and his associates could find in their magistrates and their laity a spirit of tolerance rejected by the high Calvinists. Similarly, the development of the principle of comprehension in England was accompanied by giving the laity a significant role in the church, even apart from the magistracy. Moreover, the system in itself was intended as a means of providing for greater freedom within the church as a social organization and as a household of faith. It provided an opportunity for differentiation within the established church.

But freedom of association, the freedom to form new and unhampered religious organization was not yet available—the freedom to organize independent differentiation. Before the appearance of Arminianism this freedom had been demanded in

[6] Cf. the section entitled "The Laymen and the Moderates," in W. K. Jordan, *The Development of Religious Toleration in England* (Cambridge: Harvard University Press, 1941), II, 315-491. This section provides also an account of the Arminian leaders, Arminius, Uitenbogaert, Grotius, and Episcopius.

various branches of the left wing of the Reformation. After the Synod of Dort the next phase of development in Arminianism was the struggle to secure this sort of freedom of association, the struggle of a minority excluded from the territorial church.

What is involved here is much more than the demand for freedom of faith for the individual. The demand is for the freedom of the individual to associate with others in the promotion of forms of consensus which are not shared by the total community or by the territorial church. The demand is for group freedom, for the freedom of an institution. More than that, it is the demand for the freedom of a minority group. This sort of freedom of association is a watershed between the left and the right wing of the Reformation, between territorialism and voluntarism. It is the harbinger of the modern conception of the multi-group society.

We should now trace briefly the transition to the new conception of society. Following the Synod of Dort the Arminian clergy were banished from the United Provinces. Soon thereafter Uitenbogaert, formerly court preacher at The Hague, formed this scattered group of leaders into an association or society. These men from their places of exile secretly re-entered the country. Rallying the laity, they organized the Remonstrant-Reformed congregations. Uitenbogaert retained the idea of Arminius that the group should admit differences among themselves in matters not fundamental. Thus the Remonstrants distinguished themselves from the typical sectarian group. They became a nonconforming association that permitted a degree of noncomformity within itself. That is, it made room for innovation, self-criticism, differentiation within the group. But Uitenbogaert did not wish complete independence from the state. On scriptural grounds he held that the Christian magistrate should recognize and maintain "only one religion, and no other publicly." The magistrates, however, should not be intolerant advocates of an exclusive religion. They should "permit and tolerate in their dominions, other kinds of religion, by way of connivance; looking upon them, as it were, through the fingers."

It was Episcopius who markedly advanced the Remonstrant theory of associations. Although he held that the ruler is rightly responsible for all public functions in both church and state, he insisted that everyone should be free to express his own opinion on religious matters. He denied that the acceptance of a creed should be a test of loyalty. Freedom of inquiry should be encouraged. As against the Calvinists who would permit heretics only to hold private opinions, he insisted that they be allowed freedom of association and public worship so long as they did not challenge the essential authority of the ruler and of the recognized faith. Religion should be a matter of persuasion and choice, not of coercion. No one should arrogate to himself the right to determine what are heresies. Here Episcopius anticipates the Arminian John Milton in the view that truth should be pursued in open and free encounter. To the Calvinists Episcopius suggested that they should not worry about the risks involved here. In their view the reprobates are already damned, and the elect cannot be corrupted. Curiously enough, the Calvinist Roger Williams of Rhode Island would presently also use precisely this argument to defend complete religious liberty. In the view of Episcopius intolerance exacts a great and insufferable tax. It stifles conscience, it prevents reform, it promotes hypocrisy, it even gives occasion for sedition. What an eloquent defender of these principles is Episcopius. He says:

Be unwilling, O princes, that yours should be the right from God to bespatter your crown with the blood of the erring. Let it suffice that they approve your sceptre by faith, service and other fitting duties. Religion must be defended not by slaying but by admonishing, not by ferocity but by patience, not by crime but by faith.

And then comes a sharp thrust at the Calvinists who are indulging theocratic yearnings: "We hold the power of the magistrate to be great without equal; but the orthodox cherish it as the fulcrum of theirs." And of the Calvinists who in the name of the Word of God would suppress liberty of conscience he asks, "If they stood before a king who believed differently, although upon Scriptural grounds, would not their individual conscience prove their ultimate defence?"[7] But none of these views belies the conviction of Episcopius in favor of comprehension. He favors it both before and after the Synod of Dort. Like his colleagues, he wishes the Remonstrant Brotherhood to be a part of a latitudinarian national church and not to occupy the status of a minority. Episcopius does not conceive of the Brotherhood as a free church in a free state. He remained Erastian. The idea of the free church at this period stems more from the Baptists and the Congregationalists.

Nevertheless, viewed in the context of the Calvinism of his time and place, the outlook of Episcopius is impressive. He exposed clerical pretension, and he rejected coercion in religion. He emphasized the voluntary character of religion, liberty of conscience, and freedom of inquiry. He defended the rights of freedom of association even for heretics; indeed, he adumbrated the

[7] *Vedelius Rhapsodus*, chap. ix. Quoted by Nobbs, *op. cit.*, p. 103.

civil right of such freedom of association. These are views that much of the rest of Christendom have come to accept.

It is not difficult to believe that Episcopius exercised considerable influence upon the English Independents, for his works were read in England throughout the century. The specific role, however, of Arminianism in the development of democratic thought in the New Model Army and among the Levellers is far from clear. A variety of influences seems to have played a role, and Arminianism was among these influences. In a general way and without offering documentation the British scholar A. S. P. Woodhouse affirms that it weakened the theological basis of Puritan inequalitarianism, of the conception of an aristocracy of the elect, and thus undermined "the most formidable barriers separating Puritanism from democracy."[8] We have previously noted its influence in the Church of England of the time.

For my final illustration of the effect of Arminianism upon the theory and practice of religious association I shall turn to the Methodism of two centuries later. Here, too, other influences besides those coming from Arminianism (as understood by the Methodists) belong in the picture. But there is little doubt that John Wesley's Arminian belief that God has given every man the ability to respond to the gospel and his doctrines of assurance and perfection served as the principal nerve of the development of a new ethos in British and American society. This outcome, to be sure, does not become strikingly evident until the middle

[8] *Puritanism and Liberty* (Chicago: University of Chicago Press, 1951), p. 54. Leo Solt raises a question as to whether the influence of Arminianism among the Independents was always clearly in this direction. See his *Saints in Arms* (Stanford, Calif.: Stanford University Press, 1959), p. 67.

of the nineteenth century, about three-quarters of a century after the beginning. But when these developments do come, they affect group formations at three levels, namely, within the structure of the organization of Methodism, in the relation between Methodism and the state, and in the relations between Methodism and other associations in the community.

Alfred North Whitehead has rightly affirmed that Wesley turned the energies of Britain and America in new directions, but this did not take place without dust and heat within Methodism itself. Wesley was a Tory. He required his preachers to take a loyalty oath to the crown and he frowned upon any disposition among his followers to express political interests in the name of Methodism. Nothing could seem to be less promising for dynamic, democratic politics than Wesley's outlook. Wesley, the father of Methodism, was the autocrat of Methodism. The structure of social authority within early Methodism could not have been less democratic.

Yet Wesley, with his genius for organization, devised a social invention that was to subvert his own political standpattism and his own preference for ecclesiastical hierarchy. Within each society Wesley asked that class meetings be formed. Each class meeting was composed of a dozen members who met regularly for interpersonal discipline, for self-examination, prayer, and guidance in the daily problems of the Christian life. Women as well as men played a role here, also in positions of leadership. The class meeting was not dissimilar to the *eccesiola in ecclesia* which appeared in the left wing of the Reformation and in Pietism. It provided a face-to-face dynamic fellowship, indeed a number of such fellowships, in each congregation or town. In some places there were as many as three hundred class meetings. Moreover, each of these class meetings required assignment of organizational function. Now, if we remember also that the growth of Methodism was simultaneous with the advance of the industrial revolution, that the bulk of Methodist membership came from the lower and middle classes, many of them being humble workers, it becomes readily evident why the class meeting became a great leveler, particularly as the class constituency broadened. By necessity the class meeting, and for that matter the entire structure of Methodism, required people who would assume responsibility not only as individuals in their immediate personal relationships but also as participants in the organizational structure. These developments, to be sure, gave rise to heated dispute. Nevertheless, within one or two generations these people gained a vigorous capacity to assert their freedom, indeed to exercise power in the sense of participating in social decisions. They trained themselves in the art of self-government. We cannot here detail the ways in which they change the structure of authority within the denomination, and in which they broadened the areas for individual and group participation. The whole process is another illustration of the activation of the laity and of lay preachers.[9]

Especially striking is the fact that they began to try to change the world outside the church. Under a variety of influences emanating partly from nonconformity they did four things that illustrate the role of freedom of association as a voluntary moral discipline: they became critical of the state and separated their church from the state; they became politically active in promot-

[9] Elie Halévy, *A History of the English People in the Nineteenth Century*, Vol. III: *The Triumph of Reform, 1830-41*, trans. by E. T. Watkin (2d. ed.; Gloucester, Mass.: P. Smith, 1950).

ing legislation or in impeding it; they gave leadership to the labor movement in its struggle for freedom of association and for the improvement of the human condition; and they threw their energies into other nonecclesiastical associations concerned with philanthropy and social reform—prison reform, factory legislation, and the like. Not least significant in these efforts was the Sunday school, the missionary movement, and a little earlier the antislavery movement. Besides all this the Methodist movement promoted industry, thrift, and private investment. In these ways Methodism provided a powerful religious sanction to those qualities most conducive to the building of an enterprise economy. Some scholars have suggested, accordingly, that Max Weber in his search for the psychological sources of the spirit of capitalism, should have given more attention that he did to the Methodists and to the Arminians generally. Many of these same developments appeared among the Remonstrants who pioneered in social and philanthropic causes. In the United States similar transformations took place. One can see these tendencies in American Congregationalism and Unitarianism. The Social Gospel, appearing in the late nineteenth century, reflects similar motifs which cannot be clearly distinguished from the basic thrust of theological Arminianism. Towards the middle of the nineteenth century the Unitarian William Ellery Channing, shortly after setting forth his partly Arminian objections to the five points of Calvinism, wrote on "the elevation of the laboring classes" and even on the theory of voluntary associations. In Channing's study in Boston a remarkably large number of associations for the improvement of the community were formed. Under his inspiration also the first settlement house in America was formed. These are among the most important forces that in the various countries represented at the symposium helped to create the modern democratic society insofar as it is democratic.

We have covered a wide sweep of history in this brief survey of certain of the social issues of Arminianism. This survey suggests the question: Does Arminianism give rise to a special type of Protestant, to what has been called "the Arminian man"? It is not an exaggeration to say that strict Calvinism has tended to engender fanaticism, and if not fanaticism then at least arbitrary conceptions of grace and the will of God. This quality of strict Calvinism is epitomized in a slogan that became current at the end of the Cromwellian Protectorate: "Nothing is so dangerous as a Presbyterian just off his knees." This quality is no longer characteristic in Presbyterian circles. We need not attribute the change to the moderating influence of Arminianism alone. But we can say that in the seventeenth century one sees in Holland and England the development (under the aegis of Arminianism) of a conception of God which stresses the rational, benevolent attributes and of a conception of man which mitigates the doctrine of total depravity in the direction of emphasizing the capacities for response and for disciplined responsibility in man. Here was an effort to enlarge the powers of man and to reduce the element of the arbitrary in grace. By the time these ideas were expanded during the period of the Enlightenment, "Arminianism" had revealed its characteristic danger—the interpretation of God's grace as the warranty and fulfillment of the capacities of man, with less emphasis upon the view of the Reformation and of Arminius that God's grace is required precisely in the face of human limitations and sin. In strict Calvinism the sense of the glory of God is so overpowering that it issues in heteronomy. In Enlightenment "Arminianism" the sense of human capacity is so much stressed as to approach a self-sufficient autonomy. Ernst Troeltsch's term "autotheonomy" aptly indicates the essential quality of Arminian piety—an ultimate dependency upon divine grace which does not abrogate but rather grounds, limits, and fulfills autonomy.

The shift in mentality from high Calvinism to Neo-Calvinist Arminianism, we have seen, gives rise to a different conception of associations. Whereas previously the Calvinist favored a rigidly unitary and authoritarian church, the Arminians moved in the direction of seeking greater freedom within the established church ("comprehension") and of providing room within the community for greater freedom to associate even for the promotion of heresy. The Arminian thrust in history has been in the direction of pluralism, on the presupposition that flexibility and openness make way for the appropriate reception of divine grace and for the fuller response to the gospel. Freedom within associations and freedom of associations thus became the social-organizational consequence. Troeltsch has succinctly epitomized this essential element in the Arminian striving for the "holy community." He says:

> Neo-Calvinism extends the principle of the formation of all fellowship by means of association to every relationship in life, and everywhere it manifests a tendency to form societies for ecclesiastical and religious ends, as well as for civic and cultural purposes. . . . Neo-Calvinism lays stress upon the co-operation of Christianity and Humanity in a sense quite foreign to the older Calvinism. From that standpoint it then proceeds to develop a pacifist international spirit and pacifist propaganda, champions the rights of humanity, encourages the anti-slavery movement, and allies itself with philanthropic and humanitarian movements. . . . The earnest Christian

sections of American and English Protestantism—which, in England, under the influence of the Evangelicals, includes also a large part of the State Church—represent the humane, freedom-loving, and cosmopolitan ethic of Liberalism.[10]

In both Europe and America this associational thrust gradually freed itself from the constricting bonds of Erastianism. The Erastianism was a residue of the old territorialism which held within it a quite different associational "genius" from that which was already implicit in and was already struggling for expression in Arminius and his predecessors and followers.

Taking these features into account, we may say that the Calvinist man was "an instrumental activist." He viewed himself as an instrument in the hands of the Almighty, carrying out his will in the work of the Kingdom. This Calvinist man became almost an irresistible force in the name of God. The Arminian man was aware of freedom of choice under God, and yet he was under the command to work for the holy community. Just as God had given him freedom to choose, so he felt he should give others freedom also—freedom not only to choose but freedom also to associate. It was out of this ethos that the social issues we have adumbrated came to the fore.

I have ventured to define and illustrate the social issues of Arminianism under two sociological rubrics, the principle of individuation and the principle of freedom of and in association, presupposing throughout that the theological insights of Ar-

[10] Ernst Troeltsch, *The Social Teaching of the Christian Churches,* trans. Olive Wyon (New York: The Macmillan Co., 1960), p. 675. Used by permission of The Macmillan Co. and George Allen & Unwin Ltd. For a severely critical estimate of "Arminianism" see Martin E. Marty, *The New Shape of American Religion* (New York: Harper & Brothers, 1959).

minianism delineated in the previous papers in this symposium in varying ways inform these principles. Much that has been said here is summed up in a sentence of appreciation which comes from the pen of a contemporary Roman Catholic scholar, Friedrich Heer, who says in *The Third Force,* a recent book on European spiritual history:

> Everything that has accrued on Calvinist soil, from the seventeenth to the twentieth century of the Western world, in elements of freedom, of culture of the spirit, of peace, of tolerance, of political enlightenment, and that is much, very much, is unthinkable without the movement for freedom that set in with Arminius and his spiritual affinities.[11]

It would be an egregious error, however, to suppose that the situation in which we find ourselves today is very much more favorable to Arminianism in these respects than the situation out of which it initially emerged. We today confront new forms of territorial religion and of psychic violence. What else is the religion of nationalism? Edward Shillito years ago called this the modern man's other religion. We today live in a conspicuously conformist society. What else is the world of the organization man? What else is the society dominated by the mass media of communications, media that are under the control of anonymous and powerful authorities from the Hollywood to the Madison Avenue of each country. Our churches exist within this context. Indeed, in many ways they reflect the popular piety hidden within these bulwarks of territory and class—and, we might add, of race.

In face of this situation we recall the word of Schleiermacher

---

[11] Friedrich Heer, *Die Dritte Kraft* (Frankfurt au Main: Fischer, 1959), p. 577.

that the Reformation must continue. The Arminians continued the Reformation into a third reform. In the spirit of this third Reformation we of this assembly celebrate the four-hundredth anniversary of a man who taught of the mercy as well as the judgment of God and who taught that this God who groweth not old bringeth forth treasures both new and old for those who respond to him in the responsibility that belongs to Christian liberty.

[6] Faith and Wonder

Russell Henry Stafford

"Such knowledge is too wonderful for me; it is high, I cannot attain unto it." (Ps. 139:6.)

Of all our company in the Arminius Symposium, I doubt whether any can have been more grateful than I for the illumination and refreshment which these brilliant discussions have brought us. I was brought up in the Arminian tradition, and those early influences confirmed the natural abhorrence which I take it that all who know the living Christ in the living pages of the Gospels must feel for the distinctive dogmas of Calvinism.

The mind of Arminius was a force and a source both corrective and creative in the fashioning of an evangelical theology generally acceptable in its day. Yet, as we have been thinking together through the episodes of intellect which marked the re-emergence of Christian freedom in the sixteenth century, I have found myself questioning the competence of theology, in the last instance, beyond helping us to understand our own experience, and to set forth this understanding in terms not offensive to the intelligence of others in the special idiom of our own time. No matter how much we still venerate Arminius, for example, we can no longer use his language, save within quotation marks, unless we are talking thoughtless singsong. Neither he nor any other is the definitive theologian. There can never be a definitive theology. I am induced to wonder at the limitations of man's conceptual knowledge of God, as the poet of the 139th psalm wondered at the magnitude of God's immediate and concerned knowledge of his creatures everywhere in the world he has given them.

These limitations of our understanding are displayed to our awareness when we consider that both sides in the classic Christian debates would seem to be necessarily true. Calvin declares that God has all power, of course. Arminius declares that man too has freedom. Allowing for historical and temperamental differences, they are Augustine and Pelagius over again. Both are right in principle; and in varying degrees, wrong through overemphasis. In like fashion on another issue, Athanasius and Arius, Calvin and Socinus, the Congregationalists and the Unitarians of New England in the early nineteenth century are right in what they affirm and are wrong in what they deny, at least implicitly, as to the nature of Our Blessed Lord. And so it goes. We cannot have it both ways; yet we must. For God the Father and man his child are both so wonderful that when we try to confine either within a logical construct of consecutive ideas the truth—some vital part of the whole truth—escapes through the chinks in our syllogisms.

Does that mean that we can have no theology? But as thinking Christians we must have a theology, at some points each his very own; and we must trust our several theologies for their aptness to minds of our type, yet with modest recognition of their probable inadequacy for general and exclusive acceptance. We are reminded of the scholastic tenet that all knowledge of God, and hence of man in relation with him, is by analogy. It is as if God were thus and so; yet God is more and other, also, than this analogy can convey. To know him and ourselves wholly as he and we are known to him—such knowledge is too wonderful for us; it is high, we cannot attain it.

One reason why I am happy in the fellowship of the small but irenically potent world communion in which the Remonstrant Brotherhood is an honored component is that, in its evolution, it has become the Christian body which perhaps most consistently repudiates the identification of faith with any one set of religious ideas, no matter how artfully articulated. To us in general, faith is not the mind's endorsement of convincing arguments addressed to the reason from the premises of an unique revelation, but the experience at firsthand of a supreme order of reality which is not mediated through the senses and therefore cannot be reduced without remainder to any verbal statement. It is something we either know because we cannot doubt it, or we do not know it at all; just as we know, because we cannot doubt it; that we are not dreamers adrift in a realm of phantoms but alive and awake in a real world; though, to be sure, there will always be solipsists to deny it on the surface of their minds. A communion that will accept me because I know that my Redeemer liveth, no matter how I claim to relate that allover certitude to the field of the common understanding, is the only kind of Christian company in which I can conscientiously feel at home.

But we do know that our Redeemer liveth. For we and all who are Christians in more than name have this in common: that in one man, his life and words and acts, his death and resurrection, the total impact of his personality, we have discovered the sign from heaven, the one perfect analogy. It is as if God were exactly like this man because, as we dare to say, for our faith is precisely this inescapable experience, this man is God come to earth. And as most of us find ourselves constrained to add, he is now com-present with God the Father and the Holy Spirit, ruling this world and all possible worlds of his free creatures, in the irreducible paradox of divine omnipotence and genuine responsible human liberty.

That in itself explains nothing, however. It is a completely reassuring experience for today and forever; an irresistible invitation to trustfulness which, while we remember to live in its atmosphere, must banish all anxiety and bathe us in the innocent and exultant liberty of the children of God. But it is not an explanation. Or, if you will, Jesus explains God; but who shall explain Jesus? Who can ever sound the height and depth and breadth and length of his unsearchable magnificence, shining through the shabby habiliments of his humble estate in manhood?

And that opens wide anew the door to wonder, the most exhilarating of human sensations; a door which for most men closes as childhood recedes and the hard matter of fact of daily circumstance shuts them up within a shell of private routine. Indeed, even we Christians must be at pains ever and again to break through the barriers of business, including church administration, into that mood which was Paul's when he exclaimed in ecstasy of happy bewilderment, "All things are yours; . . . And ye are Christ's; and Christ is God's." But break through we must, if our religion is to be more than a mere form of observance plus a mere code of behavior. For true religion is the celebration of faith. And faith is essentially a wonderful experience which repristinates the whole universe in its authentic, inexhaustible, inexplicable splendor before the opening eyes of our spirits.

FAITH AND WONDER

What a wonderful world we live in! And how wonderfully good it is, by night and by day, in tempest and in calm, when once in Christ we have read, marked, and inwardly digested its secret published by God himself through that one human life! Though he could know Christ only, as it were, by anticipation, yet the poet of the 139th psalm had come to the very heart of faith in that song which, reporting its author's awed and joyous bewilderment at the range and intimacy of God's knowledge, encompasses by way of illustration all lands and all seas and all creatures, and here and hereafter alike. When the sense of wonder departs, the water of life dries up in our hearts, to leave only a pathetic, sterile stain where once it freely flowed. Faith is born in wonder; it dies when wonder goes.

I am not a theologian. I have often wished that I were. I should like to flatter myself that I have a naturally theological mind. Yet, despite all the fascination of subtle arguments upon celestial themes, I have this fear of and for theologians as such: that the sheer mathematics, so to speak, of the enchanting game they play, useful and even indispensable as that game is to assuage our own qualms and to state our case to the contemporary world in terms of intellectual respectability, may imprison them under a dark roof of logic, keeping out the vitalizing radiance of God's wonderful world and the wonderful place he has given us in it. As between Calvin and Arminius, frankly I will walk in Arminius' train. But from Calvinists and Arminians alike, as from all others to whom distinctive dogmas seem of prime importance, I believe we all need, for the health of our souls, to break away now and then, and move out into the cosmic dimensions of this great psalm and many another scriptural utterance in like vein; out where the wonder of God's knowledge, and of the sun and the stars which are the work of his fingers, and of man's opportunity and destiny within this boundless dazzling horizon, breaks upon us like a returning tide, and we exclaim, not in humiliation but with the joy of filial humility, "Such knowledge is too wonderful for me; it is high, I cannot attain unto it."

BIBLIOGRAPHY

Arminian Magazine, The. Vol. I. London: 1778.

Arminius, James. *The Writings of James Arminius.* Translated by James Nichols and W. R. Bagnall. 3 vols. Grand Rapids: Baker Book House, 1956.

Bangs, Carl O. "Arminius and the Reformation Theology." Unpublished thesis, University of Chicago, 1958.

Bangs, Nathan. *Life of Arminius.* New York: Harper & Brothers, 1843.

Braithwaite, William C. *The Beginnings of Quakerism.* Second Edition. New York: Cambridge University Press, 1955.

Brandt, Casper. *The Life of James Arminius, D.D.* Translated by John Guthrie with an Introduction by Thomas O. Summers. Nashville: E. Stevenson and F. A. Owen, agents, 1857.

_____. *Life of James Arminius, D.D.* Translated by John Guthrie with an Introduction by John J. Tigert. Nashville: Publishing House of the Methodist Episcopal Church, South, 1908.

Brandt, Gerard. *The History of the Reformation and Other Ecclesiastical Transactions in and About the Low-Countries.* Translated from the Low-Dutch. 4 vols. London: T. Wood, 1720-22.

Brown, William Adams. *Christian Theology in Outline.* New York: Charles Scribner's Sons, 1906.

Cell, George Croft. *The Rediscovery of John Wesley.* New York: Henry Holt & Co., 1935.

Chesterman, A. de M. *Axholme Baptists.* Crowle, Lincolnshire: 1949.

Clarke, William N. *Outline of Christian Theology.* New York: Charles Scribner's Sons, 1898.

Colie, Rosalie Littell. *Light and Enlightenment: A Study of the Cambridge Platonists and the Dutch Arminians.* New York: Cambridge University Press, 1957.

Curtiss, George Lewis. *Arminianism in History.* Cincinnati: Cranston & Curts, 1894.

DeWolf, L. Harold. *The Case for Theology in Liberal Perspective.* Philadelphia: The Westminster Press, 1959.

Encyclopaedia Britannica. 11th Edition. New York: Encyclopaedia Britannica Company, 1910-11.

Fisher, George Park. *History of Christian Doctrine.* New York: Charles Scribner's Sons, 1896.

Fisher, Samuel. *Rusticus ad Academicos.* London: 1660.

Foster, Frank Hugh. *A Genetic History of New England Theology.* Chicago: University of Chicago Press, 1907.

Halévy, Elie. *A History of the English People in the Nineteenth Cen-*

tury (*The Triumph of Reform,* 1830-41, translated by E. T. Watkin, Vol. III.) 2d. ed; Gloucester, Mass.: P. Smith, 1950.

Hall, Thomas Cuming. *The Religious Background of American Culture.* Boston: Little, Brown & Co., 1930.

Harrison, Archibald H. W. *The Beginnings of Arminianism.* London: University of London Press, 1926.

Heer, Friedrich. *Die Dritte Kraft.* Frankfurt au Main: Fischer, 1959.

Hurst, John Fletcher. *History of the Christian Church.* 2 vols. New York: Eaton and Mains, 1897.

———. *History of Methodism.* 7 vols. New York: Eaton and Mains, 1902-4.

Jordan, W. K. *The Development of Religious Toleration in England.* Cambridge, Mass.: Harvard University Press, 1941.

Lawson, John. *Notes on Wesley's Forty-Four Sermons.* London: The Epworth Press, 1946.

Le Clerc, Jean. *Ars Critica.* 2 vols. Amstelaedami: apud Janssonio-Waesbergios, 1697.

Lindström, Harald. *Wesley and Sanctification; A Study in the Doctrine of Salvation.* Stockholm: NYA Bokförlags Aktiebolaget, 1946.

Lloyd, Sir John, and Jenkins, R. T., editors. *Dictionary of Welsh Biography down to 1940.* Oxford, England: B. H. Blackwell, Ltd., 1959.

McGiffert, Arthur Cushman. *Protestant Thought Before Kant.* New York: Charles Scribner's Sons, 1951.

McLachlan, Herbert. *The Methodist Unitarian Movement.* Manchester, England: The University Press, 1919.

Marty, Martin E. *The New Shape of American Religion*. New York: Harper & Brothers, 1959.

Motley, John Lothrop. *The History of the United Netherlands, from the Death of William the Silent to the Twelve Years' Truce—1609*. 4 vols. New York: Harper & Brothers, 1861-68.

—————. *Life and Death of John of Barneveld*. 2 vols. New York: Harper & Brothers, 1874.

—————. *The Rise of the Dutch Republic*. New York: Harper & Brothers, 1856.

Nobbs, Douglas. *Theocracy and Toleration; A Study of the Disputes in Dutch Calvinism from 1600 to 1650*. New York: Cambridge University Press, 1938.

Parrington, Vernon Louis. *Main Currents in American Thought*. New York: Harcourt, Brace & Co., 1927, 1930.

Peters, John Leland. *Christian Perfection and American Methodism*. Nashville: Abingdon Press, 1956.

Scholten, Jan Hendrik. *De Leer der Hervormde Kerk*. 2 vols. Leiden: P. Engels, 1861-62.

Shipley, David Clark. "Development of Theology in American Methodism in the Nineteenth Century," *The London Quarterly and Holborn Review* (July, 1959).

Solt, Leo F. *Saints in Arms: Puritanism and Democracy in Cromwell's Army*. Stanford, California: Stanford University Press, 1959.

Stevens, Abel. *Life and Times of Nathan Bangs, D.D.* New York: Carlton & Porter, 1863.

Stoughton, John. *History of Religion in England, from the Opening of the Long Parliament to 1850.* 8 vols. London: Hodder & Stoughton, 1881.

Summers, Thomas O. *Systematic Theology: A Complete Body of Wesleyan Arminian Divinity.* Nashville: Methodist Episcopal Church, South, 1888.

Sweet, William Warren. *The Story of Religion in America.* New York: Harper & Brothers, 1930.

Taylor, Adam. *History of the English General Baptists.* London: 1818. Vol. II.

Thomas, Joshua. *History of the Baptist Association in Wales, from 1650 to 1790.* London: 1795.

Troeltsch, Ernst. *The Social Teaching of the Christian Churches.* Translated by Olive Wyon. 2 vols. New York: The Macmillan Co., 1960.

Tyerman, L. *Life and Times of the Rev. John Wesley, M.A.,* 2nd Edition. 3 vols. New York: Harper & Brothers, 1872.

——————. *Life and Times of the Rev. Samuel Wesley, M.A.* London: Simpkin, Marshall & Co., 1866.

Underwood, Alfred Clair. *History of the English Baptists.* London: Carey Kingsgate Press, Ltd., 1947.

Warren, William Fairfield. *In the Footsteps of James Arminius.* New York: Phillips and Hunt, 1888.

Wesley, John. *A Plain Account of Christian Perfection.* Thomas S. Kepler, editor. New York: The World Publishing Co., 1954.

——————.*Forty-Four Sermons.* London: The Epworth Press, 1948.

Whitley, William Thomas, editor. *Minutes of the General Assembly of the General Baptist Churches in England*. Vol. I. 1909.

Wiley, Henry Orton. *Christian Theology*. Kansas City, Missouri: Nazarene Publishing House, 1940-43.

Williams, Daniel Day. *The Andover Liberals, a Study in American Theology*. New York: King's Crown Press, 1941.

Winebrenner, John. *History of All the Religious Denominations in the United States*. 3rd edition. Harrisburg, Pa.: John Winebrenner, V.D.M., 1853.

Woodhouse, Arthur Sutherland Pigote, editor. *Puritanism and Liberty; Being the Army Debates (1647-49) from the Clarke Manuscripts with Supplementary Documents*. 2nd edition. Chicago: University of Chicago, 1951.

INDEX

Academy at Geneva, 11, 12
Acquoy, Johannes G. R., 42
Adams, James Luther, 88
Anabaptists, 11, 91
Andrews, Launcelot, 47
Anselm of Canterbury, 37
Arianism, 50 ff, 53
Aristotle, 12
Arius, 114
Arminian Magazine, The, 47-48, 57, 74
Arminius Symposium, 64
Asbury, Francis, 73
Athanasius, 114
Augsburg Confession, 14-15
Augustine, 75, 98, 114

Bangs, Carl O., 76, 83, 96
Bangs, Nathan, 74-75
Baptist, 52, 54 ff. 60-61, 73
Baptist Missionary Society, 60
Barneveld, John of, 88, 93
Basel University, 13

Baxter, Richard, 49, 60, 74
Belgic Confession, 14, 29
Bellarmine, 17
Bertius, Peter, 12
Bèze, Théodore de, 12, 17, 82, 98
Bowne, Borden Parker, 75
Braithwaite, William C., 62, 119
Brandt, Casper, 74, 75, 84
Brandt, Gerard, 93, 94
Brethren of the Common Life, 91
Brown, William Adams, 120
Bruno, 17
Bucer, 17
Bullinger, 12, 25
Burchardt, Jakob, 93

Calvin, John, 11, 12, 14, 17, 31, 64 ff.,
    72, 78, 82, 86, 101, 114, 117
Castellio, 24
Cell, George Croft, 65-66
Channing, William Ellery, 107
Charles I, 55, 67

Charles II, 54
Chauncy, Charles, 90
Chesterman, A. de M., 54, 55
Church of England, 47, 58, 71, 73, 74, 91, 100
Church of the Nazarene, 76, 77
Coke, Thomas, 73
Colie, Rosalie L., 39, 47, 90
Congregationalism, 77, 99, 107
Coolhaes, Jasper, 97
Coornhert, 25
Cudworth, 39
Curcellaeus, Stephanus, 39, 40
Curtis, Olin A., 75

Danson, Thomas, 49
Dante, 35
Davies, James, 52
Davis, David, 51
Declaration of Independence, 83
Declaration of Sentiments, 22
Descartes, 38, 39
DeWolf, L. Harold, 76
Dort, Synod of, 29, 47, 49, 72, 90 ff., 99, 101
Dutch Reformed Church, 12, 16, 25, 28, 41

Eaton, Nathaniel, 89
Edwards, Jonathan, 90
Elector Palatine, 15
Eliot, John, 60
Embury, Philip, 72
English Platonists, 39
Enlightenment, 30, 39, 91, 108
Episcopius, Simon, 29, 50, 102 ff.
Erasmus, 11, 17, 34, 91, 94, 97
Erastianism, 110

Finney, Charles G., 77
Fisher, Samuel, 48-49, 62
Fletcher, 74
Foster, Frank Hugh, 68
Foster, Randolph S., 75
Fox, George, 61
French Revolution, 31
Freud, Sigmund, 47
Fuller, Andrew, 60

George II, 59
Goethe, 35
Gomarus, Franciscus, 18, 20, 22 ff.
Goring, Jeremy, 56
Groenewegen, H. Y., 30
Grotius, Hugo, 70, 78, 100
Grynaeus, Simon, 25
Guthrie, John, 84

Halévy, Elie, 106
Hall, Edna, 48
Hall, Thomas Cuming, 69
Harrison, Archibald H. W., 12
Heer, Friedrich, 111
Heidelberg Catechism, 14-15, 29
Hemert, Paulus van, 40
Hermes Trismegistus, 48
Hoenderdaal, Gerrit Jan, 11
Holk, Lambertus Jacobus van, 27
Hurst, John Fletcher, 74
Hyppolitus a Collibus, 15

Isaac, Daniel, 52

James I, 15
James VI, 67
Jefferson, Thomas, 83
Jenkins, R. T., 51
Jones, Jenkin, 50-51

INDEX

Jordan, W. K., 100
Junius, Franciscus, 18, 25, 82, 84
Kant, Immanuel, 40, 80
Kierkegaard, Sören, 94
Knudson, Albert C., 75
Kuenen, Abraham, 42

Lactantius, 95
Laud, Archbishop, 47, 67
Le Clerc, Jean, 38 ff., 90
Leiden University, 12, 18, 20, 22, 34, 70, 98
Lewis, Edwin, 76
Limborch, Philip van, 29, 39
Lloyd, Charles, 51
Lloyd, David, 51
Lloyd, Evan, 52
Lloyd, Sir John, 51
Locke, John, 39
London Missionary Society, 60
Luther, Martin, 11, 12, 31, 64, 66, 72, 78, 86

McGiffert, Arthur Cushman, 80
McLachlan, Herbert, 53
Manen, 42
Marburg University, 12, 13
Marty, Martin E., 110, 122
Maurice, Prince of Orange, 13, 15, 93
Mede, 39
Melanchthon, 12, 25, 90
Mennonites, 76, 91
Methodism, 46, 47, 52, 53, 56, 57, 60, 61, 65-66, 72-73, 91, 104 ff.
Methodist Quarterly Review, The, 74
Miley, John, 75
Milton, John, 102
More, 39
Motley, John Lothrop, 88-89

Newton, John, 57
Nichols, James, 15
Nobbs, Douglas, 50, 103
Norfolk, John, 54
Nuttall, Geoffrey F., 46
Nye, Philip, 50

Oglethorpe, General, 59
Oudewater, 12, 93
Owen, John, 49

Parrington, Vernon Louis, 71
Paul, the apostle, 16, 17, 44
Pelagianism, 17, 90, 114
Pelagius, 17
Perrot, Charles, 25, 97
Peters, John Leland, 77
Philip II, 11
Phillips, Benjamin, 52
Plato, 96
Presbyterian, 53, 71, 76, 99
Prinsterer, 89
Puritans, 47, 60, 67 ff., 71, 104
Pynchon, William, 70

Quakers, 48-49, 61 ff.

Rall, Harris F., 75
Ramee, Pierre de la, 13
Raymond, Miner, 75
Rees, Richard, 51
Remonstrance, 16, 28, 30, 41
Remonstrant Brotherhood, 16, 25, 29, 30, 32-33, 38, 40, 42, 43-44, 64
Remonstrant Seminary, 35, 38, 40
Renaissance, 40
Roman Catholic, 32, 69, 93, 99, 111
Romans, Epistle to the, 16

Schleiermarcher, 111
Scholten, Jan Hendrik, 41, 42
Shakespeare, 35
Shillito, Edward, 111
Shipley, David Clark, 75
Sirks, G. J., 39
Sloughton, John, 58, 59
Smith, Timothy L., 76
Smyth, John, 54
Social Gospel Movement, 85, 107
Society for Propagating the Gospel in Foreign Parts, 58
Socinianism, 50, 53, 55, 63, 89
Socinus, 23, 114
Solt, Leo, 104
Stafford, Russell Henry, 113
Stevens, Abel, 75
Stoughton, John, 123
Strawbridge, Robert, 72
Summers, Thomas O., 75
Sweet, William Warren, 67

Taylor, Adam, 55
Taylor, Dan, 56
Taylor, Nathaniel W., 77
Tertullian, 15
Theodosius, 98
Thomas, Joshua, 52
Thomas, William, 52
Thoreau, Henry David, 84
Tiele, Cornelius Petrus, 42
Tillett, Wilbur F., 75
Tombes, John, 49
Troeltsch, Ernst, 109-10
Tyerman, Luke, 55, 57, 58

Uitenbogaert, 14 ff., 21 ff., 97, 100, 101
Underwood, Alfred Clair, 56

Unitarianism, 47, 50, 51-52, 53, 71, 89, 107

Vermuyden, Cornelius, 55
Vulgate, 31

Waddington, Wilfred, 56
Ware, Henry, 89
Warren, William Fairfield, 75
Washington, George, 89
Watkins, E. T., 106
Watson, Richard, 75
Weber, Max, 107
Wesley, Charles, 59
Wesley, John, 46, 48, 53 ff., 57 ff., 61, 65, 66, 72 ff., 104-5
Wesley, Samuel, 55, 58-59
Wesley, Susannah, 57
Wesleyan Methodist Missionary Society, 61
Westminster Abbey, 59
Westminster Confession of Faith, 69
Wetstein, J. J., 40
Whedon, Daniel D., 75
Whichcote, 39
Whitehead, Alfred North, 105
Whitley, William Thomas, 54, 61
Wiley, Henry O., 76
William I, 31
William, Prince of Orange (The Silent), 11, 13, 89
Williams, Edward, 60
Williams, Moses, 52
Williams, Roger, 51, 102
Winter, Charles, 52
Woodhouse, Arthur Sutherland Pigote, 104
Wyttenbach, Daniel Albert, 40

Zwingli, 72

www.ingramcontent.com/pod-product-compliance
Lightning Source LLC
Chambersburg PA
CBHW071454160426
43195CB00013B/2099